ENLIGHTENED COURAGE

Dilgo Khyentse Rinpoche

ENLIGHTENED COURAGE

An Explanation of
Atisha's Seven Point Mind Training

Translated from the Tibetan by
the Padmakara Translation Group

Snow Lion Publications
Ithaca, New York, USA

Snow Lion Publications
P.O. Box 6483
Ithaca, NY 14851 USA

Printed in the USA

ISBN 155939-023-9

Library of Congress Cataloging-in-Publication Data

Rab-gsal-zla-ba, Dis-mgo Mkhyen-brtse, 1910—
        Enlightened courage: an explanation of Atish's Seven point mind training /
Dilgo Khyentse Rinpoche; translation from the Tibetan by Padmakara Translation
Group.
        p.   cm.
ISBN 1-55939-023-9
1. Spiritual life—Buddhism. 2. Atisa, 982-1054. 3. Rgyal-sras Throgs-med Bzan-po-
dpal, 1295-1369.
BQ7805.R33 1933
294.3'444—dc20   93-28462
                                                                         CIP

CONTENTS

I bow to the Spiritual Friends of the Supreme Vehicle,
Source of everything good in samsara and nirvana.
By the gracious Lama's blessings
May my mind be purified with the three kinds of faith.

FOREWORD

KYABJE Dilgo Khyentse Rinpoche, whose remarkable life came to an end in September 1991, was one of the foremost poets, scholars, philosophers and meditation masters of the Mahayana, Mahamudra and Great Perfection traditions of Vajrayana Buddhism. He was highly respected by thousands of students in Tibet and throughout the world.

In the summer of 1990, we had the great honour and fortune to celebrate, from 15 July to 15 August, the fifteenth anniversary of Dilgo Khyentse Rinpoche's first visit to the West. At his students' request, Rinpoche led a seminar on 'The Heart of the Buddhist Path,' with a programme including practices, teachings, empowerments and pith-instructions from all the major schools of Tibetan Buddhism. This month-long seminar took place at Rinpoche's European seat, Shechen Tennyi Dargyeling, at La Sonnerie in the Dordogne, France.

He taught on many different levels, according to the varying capacities of each individual attending his teachings, so that all might achieve ultimate inner peace and freedom. Of all the different teachings that Khyentse Rinpoche and other Lamas gave on that occasion, this teaching, Enlightened Courage, is unique and especially important. I am therefore most grateful to the Padmakara translation group and publishing team for inviting me to introduce this book.

The teaching presented here is on the Mind Training of the Indian master Atisha (982-1054) and the Tibetan master Thogmé Zangpo (1295-1369). Rinpoche taught according to his own life-long practice and experience. This teaching is the very core of the entire practice of Tibetan Buddhism, and has been the essential heart teaching of masters in all Buddhist countries for over 2500 years.

It is the threshold, the highway and the fruit of all traditions. The Gelug tradition is the gradual path of the three levels of understanding and the three main themes of the path. The Sakya tradition is the path and fruit and the preparation for the three visions. For the Kagyu tradition, in which the two streams of the Kadampa Masters' mind training lineage and Milarepa's oral transmission of the Mahamudra flow together into one, the cause is the Buddha-nature, the support is the precious human life, the impetus the spiritual masters, the skilful means their pith instructions, and the fruit the achievement of the kayas and wisdoms. The Nyingma tradition combines determination to be free from the wheel of existence by realizing its futility, certitude in the law of cause and effects of actions, altruistic awakened mind for the welfare of others, and perfect vision of all phenomena as primordially pure.

This teaching is the fruit of the experience of the masters of the past. It is adapted to our present time and can easily be incorporated into our daily lives. The benefits it brings match our greatest needs, and through it we develop a good heart, a sense of kindness, and freedom.

I would like to thank all those who made the teaching possible at the time it was given, and the Padmakara translation group and publishing team for preparing this book. I would particularly like to thank Khyentse Tulku Jigme Nüden Dorje, who tirelessly set about transcribing the teachings in Tibetan and then translating them into English; and Wulstan Fletcher, Pema Yeshe, Kristine Permild and all who contributed to the preparation and editing of the text.

May this book inspire everyone to welcome in all languages the precious teachings preserved in all their perfect purity for centuries in Tibet. This text is a small taste of that inconceivable treasury of knowledge. In the future, may there be total freedom to preserve our rightful heritage and share it with all mankind.

On the auspicious monthly commemoration of Jedrung Rinpoche (1856-1922), who was the main disciple of the first Khyentse (1820-1892) and of Kongtrul the Great (1813-1899) and became the root master of Kyabje Dudjom Rinpoche (1904-1987) and Kangyur Rinpoche (1898-1974), I pray that all the teachers' lives be long and that all their wishes for the welfare of all beings come true. May wars, famine, and all diseases and natural disasters cease to be. May Kyabje Dilgo Khyentse Rinpoche return swiftly to continue guiding us and to beat the drum of Dharma, awakening all beings into the ultimate awakened state.

Tsetrul Pema Wangyal

Saint Léon-sur-Vézère
30th day, 7th month of the Water
Monkey year 2119
(26 September 1992)

PREFACE

BODHISATTVAS are those who seek enlightenment for the sake of all other beings. Their path is the way of selflessness whereby the mind is trained to go beyond its ordinary self-centred preoccupations and anxieties and learns, by gradual degrees, to place others at the focus of its interest and concern. This altruistic attitude forms the basis and heart of all the Buddha's teaching of the Mahayana or Great Vehicle, a system of philosophical insight and meditative practice which has been described in an immense body of scriptures and commentaries. These days it is difficult to find the time to study all these detailed texts, let alone to comprehend them, and it is sometimes hard to see the wood for the trees. The Seven Point Mind Training, on the other hand, explains the Bodhisattva practice in a nutshell. It contains instructions ranging from the meditation of *tonglen* (the imaginative exchange of happiness for suffering), to practical advice on how to transform the inescapable hardships of life into aids for progress on the path.

These teachings were first brought to Tibet in the 11th century by the great Indian master Atisha, who had himself received instruction from the most accomplished teachers of his day. Atisha's principal disciple Drom-tönpa passed them on to Chekawa Yeshe Dorje, who then for the first time compiled them in written form. The transmission of the Seven Point Mind Training has continued in an unbroken lineage until the present time.

This book is the translation of a series of teachings given by Kyabje Dilgo Khyentse Rinpoche in the course of his last visit to France in the summer of 1990, slightly more than a year before he passed away in Bhutan. Basing himself on the commentary of the celebrated master Ngulchu Thogme Zangpo, Rinpoche addressed a gathering of about three hundred people in a large tent pitched in the garden of La Sonnerie, his residence in Dordogne—circumstantial details to which he refers in the course of his teaching. The fact that Rinpoche has departed from this world adds much poignancy to his words, which his many students may regard as a parting gift to them. And it is with deep gratitude to him and with earnest prayers for his swift return that we are able to offer this translation for publication. In this volume, Khyentse Rinpoche's teaching is preceded by the whole of Chekawa's root text of the Seven Point Mind Training, which also appears line by line as it is commented in the course of the work. Finally, at the end of the teaching, we have included a translation of a devotional prayer, covering the main themes of the Mind Training, composed by Jamyang Khyentse Wangpo, the first Khyentse, when he visited Atisha's residence in Tibet.

It is perhaps as well to point out that when Rinpoche gave this teaching, he was addressing a group mainly composed of Buddhist practitioners already familiar with the broad doctrinal concepts, the names and history of the tradition. Conscious of the fact that this book will reach a much wider readership, we have included footnotes and a glossary, which though not exhaustive may prove informative to readers unfamiliar with Buddhist ideas.

A recording of Rinpoche's words was transliterated and translated by Khyentse Jigme Rinpoche and edited by Wulstan Fletcher with the much appreciated help of Kristine Permild, Michal Abrams, Helena Blankleder, Anne Benson, Stephen Gethin, Charles Hastings and John Canti, all of the Padmakara Translation Group.

ATISHA DIPAMKARA (982–1054)

THE ROOT TEXT

THE SEVEN POINT MIND TRAINING

by

Chekawa Yeshe Dorje

THE ROOT TEXT

First study the preliminaries.

Consider all phenomena as a dream.
Analyse the unborn nature of awareness.
The antidote will vanish of itself.
The nature of the path rests in the alaya.
In post-meditation, consider phenomena as illusory.
Train to give and take alternately;
Mount them both upon your breath.
Three objects, three poisons and three roots of virtue.
In all your actions, train yourself with maxims.
Begin the training sequence with yourself.

When all the world is filled with evils,
Place all setbacks on the path of liberation.
Lay the blame for everything on one.
Reflect upon the kindness of all beings.
Voidness is the unsurpassed protection;
Thereby illusory appearance is seen as the four kayas.
The best of methods is to have four practices.
To bring the unexpected to the path,
Begin to train immediately.

The pith instructions briefly summarized:
Put the five strengths into practice.
On how to die, the Mahayana teaches
These five strengths. It matters how you act.

All Dharma has a single goal.
Rely upon the better of two witnesses.
Always be sustained by cheerfulness.
With experience you can practise even when distracted.

Always train in three common points.
Change your attitude and maintain it firmly.
Do not discuss infirmities.
Do not have opinions on other people's actions.
Work on the strongest of your defilements first.
Give up hoping for results.
Give up poisoned food.
Do not be hidebound by a sense of duty.
Do not meet abuse with abuse.
Do not wait in ambush.
Do not strike at weaknesses.
Do not lay the dzo's burden on an ox's back.
Do not praise with hidden motives.
Do not misuse the remedy.
Do not bring a god down to the level of a demon.
Do not take advantage of suffering.

Do everything with one intention.
Apply one remedy in all adversity.
Two things to be done, at the start and at the finish.
Bear whichever of the two occurs.
Even if it costs you your life, defend the two.
Train yourself in three hard disciplines.
Have recourse to three essential factors.
Meditate on three things that must not deteriorate.

Three things maintain inseparably.
Train impartially in every field;
Your training must be deep and all-pervading.
Always meditate on what is unavoidable.
Do not be dependent on external factors.
This time, do what is important.
Do not make mistakes.
Be consistent in your practice.
Be zealous in your training.
Free yourself by analysis and testing.
Don't take what you do too seriously.
Do not be bad tempered.
Do not be temperamental.
Do not expect to be rewarded.

This distilled essence of instruction,
Which transmutes the upsurge of the five degenerations
Into the path of enlightenment,
Was handed down by Serlingpa.
Having roused the karma of past training,
And feeling powerfully inspired,
I disregarded suffering and censure
And sought out the instructions to subdue my ego-clinging;
Though I may die, I shall now have no regret.

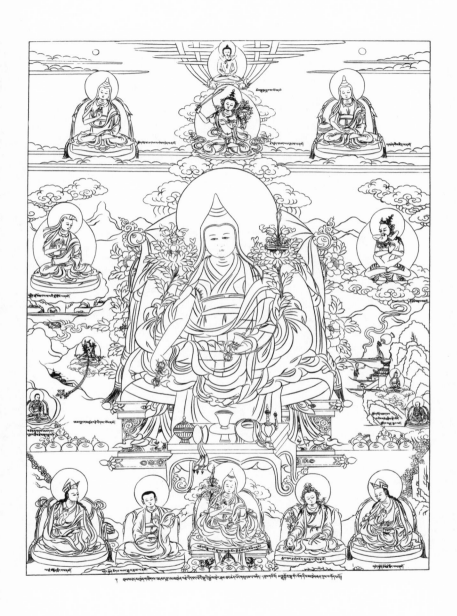

JAMYANG KHYENTSE WANGPO (1820–1892)

THE TEACHING

INTRODUCTION

Homage to Chenrezig,[1] the Great, the Compassionate!

Perfect in the threefold training
And accomplished in the twofold Bodhichitta,
You spread the teachings of the Buddha everywhere;
Crowning glory of the holders of the Doctrine,
Incomparable Master, to you I bow!

The only path of Buddhas, past, present and to come,
The treasure ground of every good and joy,
Following the words of my own master,
This doctrine I will now explain,
Requested frequently by fortunate disciples.

ALL who wish to attain supreme and unsurpassable enlightenment should strive to practise both relative and absolute Bodhichitta.

The many teachings of the Kadampa masters have been set forth in elaborate, medium and condensed form, yet the essence of them all is to be found in this text, the *Seven Points for Training the Mind*, written by the glorious Bodhisattva, Ngulchu Thogme Zangpo.[2]

In the past, in the days when the Dharma still flour-
ished in India, the communities of the Shravakayana and
the Mahayana practised separately; the Mahayana doctrine was not taught to Shravakayana assemblies. This
was not because the teachers had anything against the
followers of the Shravakayana; it was just that if the
Mahayana had been taught in such a setting, it would
have had no effect on the minds of the listeners, who
would have taken it wrongly. The Mahayana was therefore kept secret and it was only later, through the power
of Guru Rinpoche's[3] blessings, that it became possible for
the entire Dharma of the Sutrayana and Mantrayana to
be spread openly in Tibet, the Land of Snow. It is therefore
entirely due to Guru Rinpoche's kindness that, having
entered the Buddhadharma, embraced the vows of refuge, and conceived the wish that all beings might be
protected by the Triple Jewel, we now find ourselves
today upon the Mahayana path.

The Mahayana has two aspects, the profound and the
vast. The profound is explained in the Abhisamayalan-
kara and the vast in the Uttaratantra, two texts which
correspond to the second and third turnings of the wheel
of the Dharma. Both however are condensed in the Sutra-
alankarashastra, which sets forth the vast and ocean-like
activities of the Bodhisattvas. A very lengthy exposition
of all this could be given by learned masters, but in brief,
we may regard the profound and vast aspects of the
Mahayana as contained within the practice of the two
kinds of Bodhichitta, the relative and the absolute.

Relative Bodhichitta is practised on the basis of the
ordinary, conceptual mind and is perfectly possible to
accomplish, even for a beginner, provided he looks within himself and practises properly. When this relative
Bodhichitta has been perfected, moreover, absolute
Bodhichitta, the wisdom of Vipashyana, the realization

of no-self, arises by itself. This is what the Kagyupas call Mahamudra and the Nyingmapas call Dzogchen— practices which, for the moment, lie beyond our scope. For if little babies, still being fed on milk, were to be given solid food such as fruit, rice or meat, they would be unable to digest it; likewise absolute Bodhichitta is not something that we can engage in from the very first. For this reason, we must begin with the practice of relative Bodhichitta.

It was once said by Nagarjuna:[4]

> If we, ourselves and all the world,
> Should wish for unsurpassable enlightenment,
> Its basis is a Bodhichitta
> Stable as the lord of mountains:
> Compassion reaching out to all directions,
> And Wisdom that transcends duality.

We can think of relative Bodhichitta as having two aspects: that of emptiness and that of compassion. If we are grounded in the practice of compassion, we will not stray into the paths of the Shravakas and Pratyeka-buddhas; and if we rely upon the view of emptiness, we will not wander in the three realms of samsara. Perfect enlightenment, in fact, is free from both samsara and nirvana. To possess both compassion and an understanding of emptiness, is like having wheels on one's car. If all four are present, the car is roadworthy; but if a wheel is missing, it is impossible to go anywhere. Meditation on emptiness without compassion is not the Mahayana path; meditation on compassion where the aspect of emptiness is lacking is not the path either. We need both emptiness and compassion together.

The instructions of the Seven Point Mind Training originated with the three great teachers of Lord Atisha:[5] Guru Maitriyogin, who could really take upon himself the sufferings of others; Guru Dharmarakshita, who realized the nature of emptiness by meditating on love and compassion even to the point of giving away his own flesh; and Guru Dharmakirti, who lived in Serling, the Isle of Gold (nowadays part of Indonesia), and who devoted his whole life to the practice of Bodhichitta.

There is a story that one day, when Maitriyogin was teaching, a dog barked at someone, who, losing his temper, threw a stone at it. The dog was hit in the ribs and yelped. Feeling great sorrow for the animal, the teacher cried out and fell down from the throne. 'This is taking things a bit too far,' thought his disciples. Knowing what was in their minds, Maitriyogin said, 'Look here, at my ribs.' And on his body, exactly where the stone had hit the dog, he had a bruise. He had taken the suffering of the animal upon himself.

On another occasion, when Dharmarakshita was at the university of Nalanda, there was a man who was very sick, his strength completely gone. The doctors had told him that there was nothing they could do to cure him; the only possible remedy was to find the flesh of a living person. The patient was very depressed, wondering how on earth he might come by such a thing. When he heard about this, Dharmarakshita said to the man, 'If it will cure your disease, you can have my flesh.' Thereupon, he cut a piece of flesh from his thigh and gave it to the sick man, who ate it and was completely cured. Now at that time, Dharmarakshita had not yet realized the nature of emptiness and so the wound was extremely painful, especially that night in the monastery when he lay down to sleep. Nevertheless, despite the pain, the thought never crossed his mind that he had done something excessive, and he experienced not the slightest regret. As dawn approached, he fell into a light sleep and dreamed that there appeared to him a youth, shining white and very handsome.

The boy said: 'This is the kind of Bodhisattva activity we should perform for the sake of living beings. How painful is your wound?'

When Dharmarakshita replied, the boy, who was in fact Chenrezig, passed his hand over the wound and blew gently on it. Dharmarakshita thus received his blessing. When he awoke, the cut was completely healed and free from pain, and he had realized the nature of emptiness.

Dharmakirti lived close to the sea and was also known as Guru Serlingpa, the Guru of the Golden Isle. Atisha stayed with him for twelve years practising his instructions, with the result that Bodhichitta took firm root in him. Ever after, although he had many teachers and had the habit of joining his hands at his heart whenever their names were mentioned, on hearing the name of Serlingpa, he would join his hands at the crown of his head and weep. He would celebrate the anniversary of all his other teachers every year, but the passing away of Serlingpa he would commemorate every month. His disciples used to ask him, 'You seem to express your respect so differently towards your other teachers. Is that because there was a difference in their wisdom?'

'All my teachers without exception,' Atisha answered, 'attained the supreme state. Not one of them was an ordinary being, there was no difference in their qualities. Yet it is thanks to Serlingpa that Bodhichitta has taken root in me. And so there is a difference in my gratitude.'

The tradition of Serlingpa encompasses also the teaching of Maitriyogin and Dharmarakshita. There are many ways of explaining it, but following the practice of the Kadampa master Chekawa Yeshe Dorje,[6] it is set forth in verse as The Seven Point Mind Training.

I

THE BASIS FOR THE PRACTICE OF BODHICHITTA

First study the preliminaries.

AS a preliminary to this teaching, we must consider three things: the preciousness of being born a human being, the fact of impermanence and the problem of samsaric existence.

Human birth

We are at the moment in possession of a precious human existence endowed with eighteen characteristics which are very difficult to obtain. If the teachings of the Buddha are practised correctly, then it is as the saying goes:

> Used well, this body is a ship to liberation,
> Otherwise it is an anchor in samsara.
> This body is the agent of all good and evil.

From the point of view of one who seeks enlightenment, it is far better to be a human being than to be born even in the heavens of the gods, where there is nectar to live on and all wishes are granted by the wish-fulfilling tree; where there is neither fatigue nor difficulty, neither sickness nor old age. It is as humans, possessed of the eight freedoms and the ten endowments, and not as gods, that every one of the thousand Buddhas of this age has

attained, or will attain, enlightenment. This human existence, moreover, is not to be achieved by force or mere
chance; it is the result of positive actions. And because it
is rare for beings to accomplish positive actions, a precious human existence is indeed difficult to obtain. Nevertheless, we have now managed to be born into such a
state; we have encountered the Buddhadharma, have
entered the path and are now receiving teachings. But if
we are unable to practise them, simply listening to the
teachings will not in itself liberate us from samsara, and
will be of no help to us when we are confronted by the
hardships of birth, disease, old age and death. If we do
not follow the doctor's prescription when we are sick,
then even if the doctor sits constantly by our side, the pain
will not go away.

Impermanence

As we have just said, if we neglect to practise the
teachings, they will be of no use to us. Moreover our lives
are fragile and impermanent, and because death and its
causes are uncertain, we may succumb at any moment.
We may think, 'Oh, I will practise when I am older, but
now while I am young, I will live an ordinary life, making
money, getting the better of my rivals, helping my
friends, and so on.' But the fact is that we might not live
to be very old. Just think for example of the people who
were born at the same time as ourselves. Some might have
died as children, some as adults, at their work and so on.
Our own lives might not be very long either.

Furthermore, a human existence, in comparison with
that of an animal, seems almost impossible to achieve. If you
examine a clod of earth in summer, you might find more
creatures in it than the population of the whole of France!
That is why we say that, in terms of numbers alone, a
human birth is difficult to obtain. So we should make up

our minds that we will practise the Dharma instead of throwing our lives away in meaningless activities.

To use our human lives to accomplish the Buddha-dharma, is like crossing the ocean in search of costly jewels and afterwards returning home with every kind of precious thing; the difficulties of the trip will have been well rewarded. It would be a shame to come back empty-handed! We are now in possession of a precious human form and have discovered the Teachings of Buddha. Through the blessings and kindness of the teachers it is now possible for us to receive, study and practise the Doctrine. But if we are preoccupied only with the worldly activities of this life: business, farming, prevailing over enemies, helping friends, hoping for an important position and so on—and we die before we have made time for spiritual practice, it would be just like coming home empty-handed from the isle of jewels. What an incredible waste! Therefore we should think to ourselves, 'I am not going to miss my chance. While I have this precious opportunity, I will practise the Dharma.' Of course, the best thing would be to practise for the whole of our lives; but at least we should take refuge properly, for this is the essence of the Buddhadharma and closes the door to the lower realms. It is the universal antidote that can be applied in any kind of difficulty, and to practise it is therefore most important.

Although, for the moment, you do not understand me, due to the difference of our languages, you are all aware that I am giving you some instruction. After I have gone, everything will be translated for you and perhaps you will think, 'That Lama taught us something important; I must put it into practice.' If you really do so, in your lives from day to day, then my explanation will have had some point to it. So please take it to heart.

The defects of samsara

The experience of happiness and suffering comes about as the result of positive and negative actions; therefore evil should be abandoned and virtue cultivated as much as possible.

Even the tiniest insect living in the grass wishes to be happy. But it does not know how to gather the causes of happiness, namely positive actions, nor how to avoid the cause of suffering, which is evil behaviour. When animals kill and eat each other, they instinctively commit negative actions. They wish for happiness, but all they do is to create the causes of their misery and experience nothing but suffering. This is the measure of their ignorance and delusion. But if the truth were really shown to them, then without a care even for their lives, they would accomplish that very virtue which they would recognize as the source of their own happiness. The essence of the Buddha's teaching is to understand clearly what behaviour is to be adopted and what is to be rejected.

> Abandon evil-doing,
> Practise virtue well,
> Subdue your mind:
> This is Buddha's teaching.

At the moment, we are all caught in the state of delusion, and so we should acknowledge all the negative actions we have perpetrated throughout our many lives until the present time. And from now on, we should turn away from all such actions big or small, just as we would avoid getting thorns in our eyes. We should constantly be checking what we do: any negative action should be confessed immediately, and all positive actions dedicated to others. To the best of our ability, we should abandon wrongdoing and try to accumulate goodness.

II

BODHICHITTA

BODHICHITTA is the unfailing method for attaining enlightenment. It has two aspects, relative and absolute. Relative Bodhichitta is practised using ordinary mental processes and is comparatively easy to develop. Nevertheless, the benefits that flow from it are immeasurable, for a mind in which the precious Bodhichitta has been born will never again fall into the lower realms of samsara. Finally, all the qualities of the Mahayana Path, as teeming and vast as the ocean, are distilled and essentialized in Bodhichitta, the mind of enlightenment.

We must prepare ourselves for this practice by following the instructions in the sadhana of Chenrezig, 'Take refuge in the Three Jewels and meditate on Bodhichitta. Consider that all your virtuous acts of body, speech and mind are for the whole multitude of beings, numerous as the sky is vast.'

It is said in the teachings that, 'Since beings are countless, the benefit of wishing them well is unlimited.' And how many beings there are! Just imagine, in this very lawn there might be millions and millions of them! If we wish to establish them all in the enlightened state of Buddhahood, it is said that the benefit of such an aspiration is as vast as the number of beings is great. Therefore we should not restrict our Bodhichitta to a limited number of beings. Wherever there is space, beings exist, and all of them live in suffering. Why make distinctions between them, welcoming some as loving friends and excluding others as hostile enemies?

Throughout the stream of our lives, from time without beginning until the present, we have all been wandering in samsara, accumulating evil. When we die, where else is there for us to go to but the lower realms? But if the wish and thought occur to us that we must bring all beings to the enlightened state of Buddhahood, we have generated what is known as Bodhichitta in intention. We should then pray to the teacher and the yidam deities that the practice of the precious Bodhichitta might take root in our hearts. We should recite the seven branch prayer from the Prayer of Perfect Action, and, sitting upright, count our breaths twenty-one times without getting mixed up or missing any, and without being distracted by anything. If we are able to count our breaths concentratedly for a whole mala, discursive thoughts will diminish and the practice of relative Bodhichitta will be much easier. This is how to become a suitable vessel for meditation.

Absolute Bodhichitta

Consider all phenomena as a dream.

If we have enemies, we tend to think of them as permanently hostile. Perhaps we have the feeling that they have been the enemies of our ancestors in the past, that they are against us now and that they will hate our children in the future. Maybe this is what we think, but the reality is actually quite different. In fact, we do not know where or what we were in our previous existences, and so there is no certainty that the aggressive people we now have to contend with were not our parents in former lives! When we die, we have no idea where we will be reborn and so there is no knowing that these enemies of ours might not become our mothers or fathers. At present, we might have every confidence in our parents who are so dear to us, but when they go from this life, who is to say that they will not be reborn among our enemies? Because our past and future lives are unknown to us, we have the impression that the enemies we have now are fixed in their hostility, or that our present friends will always be friendly. This only goes to show that we have never given any real thought to this question.

If we consider this carefully, we might picture a situation where many people are at work on some elaborate project. At one moment, they are all friends together, feeling close, trusting and doing each other good turns. But then something happens and they become enemies, perhaps hurting or even killing one other. Such things do happen, and changes like this can occur several times in the course of a single lifetime—for no other reason than that all composite things or situations are impermanent.

This precious human body, supreme instrument though it is for the attainment of enlightenment, is itself a transient phenomenon. No one knows when, or how, death will come. Bubbles form on the surface of the water, but the next instant they are gone, they do not stay. It is just the same with this precious human body we have managed to find. We take all the time in the world before engaging in the practice, but who knows when this life of ours will simply cease to be? And once our precious human body is lost, our mindstream, continuing its existence, will take birth perhaps among the animals, or in one of the hells or god realms where spiritual development is impossible. Even life in a heavenly state, where all is ease and comfort, is a situation unsuitable for practice, on account of the constant dissipation and distraction that are a feature of the gods' existence.

At present, the outer universe—earth, stones, mountains, rocks and cliffs—seems to the perception of our senses to be permanent and stable, like the house built of reinforced concrete which we think will last for generations. In fact, there is nothing solid to it at all; it is nothing but a city of dreams.

In the past, when the Buddha was alive surrounded by multitudes of Arhats and when the teachings prospered, what buildings must their benefactors have built for them! It was all impermanent; there is nothing left to see now but an empty plain. In the same way, at the universities of Vikramashila and Nalanda,[7] thousands of panditas spent their time instructing enormous monastic assemblies. All impermanent! Now, not even a single monk or volume of Buddha's teachings are to be found there.

Take another example from the more recent past. Before the arrival of the Chinese Communists, how many monasteries were there in what used to be called Tibet, the Land of Snow? How many temples and monasteries were there, like those in Lhasa,[8] at Samye and Trandruk? How many precious objects were there, representations of the Buddha's Body, Speech and Mind? Now not even a statue remains. All that is left of Samye is something the size of this tent, hardly bigger than a stupa. Everything was either looted, broken or scattered, and all the great images were destroyed. These things have happened and this demonstrates impermanence.

Think of all the lamas who came and lived in India, such as Gyalwa Karmapa, Lama Kalu Rinpoche and Kyabje Dudjom Rinpoche; think of all the teachings they gave, and how they contributed to the preservation of the Buddha's doctrine. All of them have passed away. We can no longer see them and they remain only as objects of prayer and devotion. All this is because of impermanence. In the same way we should try to think of our fathers, mothers, children and friends... When the Tibetans escaped to India, the physical conditions were too much for many of them and they died. Among my acquaintances alone, there were three or four deaths every day. That is impermanence. There is not one thing in existence that is stable and lasts.

If we have an understanding of impermanence, we will be able to practise the sacred teachings. But if we continue to think that everything will remain as it is, then we will be just like rich people still discussing their business projects on their deathbeds! Such people never talk about the next life, do they? It goes to show that an appreciation of the certainty of death has never touched their hearts. That is their mistake, their delusion.

What is delusion? How shall we define it? It is just as when a madman runs outside on a cold winter's day and jumps into the water to wash himself, too deranged to realize that his body is being frozen. We think that such a man is insane, but in exactly the same way, when a Bodhisattva, clear-minded and undeceived, looks at us, our activities seem to him as demented as those of the lunatic! We should be quite convinced that we are thoroughly deluded and that when things appear to us the way they do, separate from our minds, they do not possess the slightest degree of reality in themselves.

But what is it that creates this illusion? It is the mind, and it does so when it takes as real that which is illusory and non-existent. Nevertheless, we should clearly understand that such delusion is actually quite distinct from the mind in itself, the Buddha-nature or Sugatagarbha; it is not something, therefore, which it is impossible for us to remove.

But what about the mind, this creator of illusion? Can even the mind itself be said to exist? To understand this, we must

Analyse the unborn nature of awareness.

When anger arises in what we think of as our minds, we become oblivious even to the dangers that might threaten us. Our faces flushed with rage, we seize our weapons and could even kill a lot of people. But this anger is an illusion; it is not at all some great force that comes rushing into us. It achieves one thing only and that is to send us to hell, and yet it is nothing but thought, insubstantial thought. It is only thought, and yet...

Take another example, that of a wealthy person. He is rich and happy and is deeply pleased with himself, thinking, 'I am rich.' But then if all his property is confiscated by an official or some such person, his happiness evaporates and he falls into depression and misery. That joy is mind. That sadness is mind. And that mind is thought.

What shall we say about these so-called thoughts? At this moment, while I am teaching Dharma, let us consider the mental experience, or thought, which you have, of listening carefully to me. Does this have a form or colour? Is it to be found in the upper or lower part of the body, in the eyes or the ears? What we call the mind is not really there at all. If it is truly some*thing*, it must have characteristics, such as colour. It must be white, yellow, etc. Or it must have shape like a pillar or a vase. It must be big or small, old or young, and so on. You can find out whether the mind exists or not by just turning inwards and reflecting carefully. You will see that the mind does not begin, or end, or stay, anywhere; that it has no colour or form and is to be found neither inside nor outside the body. And when you see that it does not exist as any *thing*, you should stay in that experience without an attempt to label or define it.

When you have truly attained the realization of this emptiness, you will be like the venerable Milarepa[9] or Guru Rinpoche, who were unaffected by the heat of summer or the cold of winter, and who could not be burned by fire or drowned in water. In emptiness there is neither pain nor suffering. We, on the other hand, have not understood the empty nature of the mind and so, when bitten by even a small insect, we think, 'Ouch! I've been bitten. It hurts!'; or when someone says something unkind, we get angry. That is the sign that we have not realized the mind's empty nature.

All the same, even granted that we are convinced that our body and mind are by nature empty, when this very conviction, which is normally called the antidote, arises in our minds, it is said, nevertheless, that:

The antidote will vanish of itself.

People who ask for Dharma teachings do so because they are afraid of what might happen to them after death. They decide that they must take refuge, request the lama for instruction and concentrate unwaveringly on the practice: a hundred thousand prostrations, a hundred thousand mandala offerings, recitations of the refuge formula and so on. These, of course, are positive thoughts, but thoughts, being without substantial nature, do not stay for very long. When the teacher is no longer present and there is no one to show what should and should not be done, then for most practitioners it is as the saying goes: Old yogis getting rich; old teachers getting married. This only goes to show that thoughts are impermanent, and we should therefore bear in mind that any thought or antidote—even the thought of emptiness—is itself by nature empty without substantial existence.

The nature of the path rests in the alaya.

But how are we to rest in emptiness, free from all mental activity? Let us begin by saying that the state of mind of thinking 'I'—has no reality whatever. Be that as it may, we do have the feeling of something real and solid which we call 'I,' and which is supported by a body with its five sense powers and eight consciousnesses. These are technical terms and are not very easy to understand. But, for example, when the eye apprehends a form, sight occurs by virtue of the eye-consciousness. If the form is something pleasant we think, 'This is good, I like it.' If we see something frightening, a ghost, for instance, or someone with a gun ready to shoot us, we think that we are going to be killed and react with horror. The truth is, however, that those outer events apparently happening 'over there' are in fact occurring 'here,' 'within;' they are fabricated by our minds.

As to where our minds are now situated, we may say that they are linked to our bodies and that it is thanks to this combination that we have the faculty of speech. A tent, pulled by ropes from the sides, and with a pole in the middle, becomes a place where we can stay. In the same way, our body, speech and mind are temporarily together. But when we die, and our minds enter the bardo, our bodies will be left behind and our speech will completely cease to exist. Our minds, moreover, will not be accompanied by the wealth we have gathered during our lives, nor by our fathers or mothers, nor by our relatives or friends. We will be alone, saddled with whatever good and evil we have done, and which we cannot shake off any more than we can get rid of our own shadows.

The body left behind at death is called a corpse. Whether it is the body of our parents or the relics of our teacher, it is just a corpse. Now, though corpses have eyes, they cannot see; they cannot hear with theirs ears or speak with their mouths. We may treat them with respect, dressing them in brocade robes and putting them on thrones; or we may treat them roughly, burning them in the fire or throwing them into water. It is all the same to the corpses. They are mindless and like stones, neither happy nor sad.

When the mind is positive, body and speech, the servants of the mind, will of course be positive also. But how are we to make the mind positive? At the moment we cling to the notion that our minds are real entities. When someone helps us, we think, 'That person has been so good to me. I must be kind to him in return and make him my friend for lives and lives to come.' This only goes to show that we do not know about the empty nature of the mind. As for our enemies, we think of how to harm them as much as possible, at best killing them or at least robbing them of all their belongings. We think like that simply because we think our anger is a true and permanent reality—while in fact it is nothing at all. We should therefore rest in the empty nature of the mind beyond all mental elaborations, in that state which is free from clinging, a clarity which is beyond all concepts.

To bring this description of absolute Bodhichitta to a conclusion, the root text says:

> In post-meditation, consider phenomena as
> illusory.

It is said that when one arises from meditation, all phenomena, oneself and others, the universe and its inhabitants, appear in the manner of an illusion. This however should be properly understood.

When great Bodhisattvas come into the world to accomplish the benefit of beings by establishing them on the path to liberation, it is not through the power of their karma or defiled emotions that they do so. As we read in the stories of his previous lives, Lord Buddha, while still a Bodhisattva, took birth among the birds and deer and so forth, in order to teach and set them on the path of virtue. He was born too as a universal ruler who practised great generosity, and later in his quest for the Dharma, for the sake of hearing only a few lines of teaching, he would burn his body, or jump into fire or water, unconcerned for his life. Because he had realized emptiness, he experienced no suffering at all. Until we achieve the same degree of realization, however, and for as long as we hold onto the idea that everything is permanent and stable, that will not be the case for us. This is something we should bear in mind as we go about our daily lives.

Relative Bodhichitta

We will consider the practice of relative Bodhichitta first as meditation, then in terms of day to day living.

With regard to meditation, it is said in the root verses that we should

Train to give and take alternately;

This refers to an extremely important practice. As the great master Shantideva[10] said,

> Whoever wishes quickly to become
> A refuge for himself and others,
> Should undertake this sacred mystery:
> To take the place of others, giving them his own.

We attach great importance to what we conceive of as *I, myself*, and therefore to such thoughts as *my* body, *my* mind, *my* father, *my* mother, *my* brother, *my* sister, *my* friend. But the concept of *others* we neglect and ignore. We may indeed be generous to beggars and give food to those who need it, but it is a fact that we do not care for them as much as we care for ourselves. This however is precisely what we should do; and conversely, just as we are now able to ignore others, we should be able to ignore ourselves. This is how Bodhichitta begins to grow; this is the extraordinary secret pith instruction of the Bodhisattvas. At the moment, this Bodhichitta has not yet awakened in myself and so it is extremely fortunate for me that I can explain it on the basis of this text.

If through listening to this explanation of the Seven Point Mind Training we come to recognise how important Bodhichitta is, this will be an infallible cause of our enlightenment. Of all the eighty four thousand different sections of the doctrine, the precious Bodhichitta is the very essence. By hearing the words of such a teaching, it is impossible even for demons, whose nature it is to kill and to do harm, not to have positive thoughts! Kham, a region in East Tibet, was haunted in the past by many ghosts and evil spirits,[11] and this was one of the reasons why Patrul Rinpoche[12] used to explain the *Bodhicharya-vatara*[13] continually to his disciples. Before long, there were no more ghosts—or at least, no one came to any more harm. Such is the hidden power of Bodhichitta!

> If I do not give away
> My happiness for others' pain,
> Buddhahood will never be attained
> And even in samsara, joy will fly from me.

Enlightenment will be ours when we are able to care for others as much as we now care for ourselves, and ignore ourselves to the same extent that we now ignore others. Even if we had to remain in samsara, we should be free from sorrow. For as I have said, when the great Bodhisattvas gave away their heads and limbs, they felt no sadness at the loss of them.

Once, in one of his previous lifetimes, the Buddha was a universal monarch whose custom it was to give away his wealth without regret. He refused nothing to those who came to beg from him and his fame spread far and wide. One day, a wicked Brahmin[14] beggar came before the king and addressed him saying, 'Great king, I am ugly to look upon, while you are very handsome; please give me your head.' And the king agreed. Now his queens and ministers had been afraid that he might do this, and making hundreds of heads out of gold, silver and precious stones, they offered them to the beggar.

'Take these heads,' they pleaded, 'do not ask the king for his.'

'Heads made of jewels are of no use to me,' the beggar replied, 'I want a human head.' And he refused to take them.

Eventually they could no longer deter him from seeing the king.

The king said to him, 'I have sons and daughters, queens and a kingdom, but no attachment do I have for any of them. I will give you my head at the foot of the tsambaka tree in the garden. If I can give you my head today, I shall have completed the Bodhisattva act of giving my head for the thousandth time.'

And so, at the foot of the tree, the king took off his clothes, tied his hair to a branch and cut off his head. At that moment, darkness covered the earth and from the sky came the sound of the gods weeping and lamenting, so loudly that even human beings could hear them. The queens, princes and ministers, all fell speechless to the ground. Then Indra, the lord of the gods, appeared and said, 'O king, you are a Bodhisattva and have even given away your head, but here I have the life-restoring ambrosia of the gods. Let me anoint you with it and bring you back to life.'

Now the king was indeed a Bodhisattva and, even though his head had been cut off and sent away, his mind was still present and he replied that he had no need of Indra's life-restoring ambrosia, for he could replace his head simply by the force of his own prayers.

Indra begged him to do so and the king said: 'If in all those thousand acts of giving my head away beneath the tsambaka tree there was nothing but the aim of benefiting others, unstained by any trace of self seeking—if I was without resentment or regret, then may my head be once again restored. But if regrets there were, or evil thoughts, or intentions not purely for the sake of others, then may my head remain cut off.' No sooner had the king said this than there appeared on his shoulders a new head identical to the first, which had been taken by the Brahmin. Then all the queens, princes and ministers rejoiced and administered the kingdom in accordance with the Dharma.

For those who can practise generosity like this, there is no suffering at all. Enlightened teachers, Bodhisattvas, come into the world to accomplish the welfare of beings, and even when they are ignored by people in the grip of desire, anger and ignorance, who stir up obstacles and difficulties, the thought of giving up never occurs to them and they are totally without anger or resentment. As it is said:

> To free yourself from harm
> And others from their sufferings,
> Give away yourself for others,
> Guard others as you would protect yourself.

Now, when training in giving away your happiness to others, it is unwise to try to give to all beings right from the start. For beings are countless and your meditation will not be stable, with the result that you will derive no

benefit from the practice. Therefore, visualize in front of
you a specific person, someone whom you love, your
mother for example. Reflect that when you were very
little, she suffered while she carried you in her womb; she
was unable to work or eat comfortably, unable even to
stand up and sit down without difficulty. Yet all the time
she loved and cared for you. When you were born from
her womb, were it not for the fact that you were actually
breathing, you could scarcely have been called a living
thing at all. You were not even strong enough to raise
your head. Nevertheless your mother took you, this little
thing which did not even know her, upon her lap to wash,
clean and bring up lovingly. Later she put up with loss
and disgrace on account of your misbehaviour, her only
preoccupation being how to keep you alive. If your parents were practitioners they introduced you, when you
were old enough, to the Dharma and to the lamas from
whom you received instruction.

In fact, it is thanks to your mother that your precious
human life exists at all. If she had not been there, who
knows whether you would have attained it? Therefore you
should be very grateful to her. Thinking in terms not only
of this but of countless lives, understand that all beings
have been your mothers and have cared for you just as
your present mother has done. When your mother looks
at you, she does not frown, but looks at you with loving
eyes. Calling you her dear child, she has brought you up,
protecting you from heat and cold and all the rest. In every
way she has tried to bring about your happiness. Even if
she could give you the kingdom of a universal ruler, she
would still not be satisfied and would never think that
she had given you enough. Your mother, therefore, is
someone to whom you should have an endless gratitude.

If, on growing up, someone abandons his aged and
sick parents instead of caring for them, people think of

him as shamelessly ungrateful, and rightly so. But even if we are not like that, it is absurd to say that we respect our parents, while caring only for ourselves. On the other hand, if we do look after them, but supply them only with material things: food, clothing, even the wealth of a whole country, they would be benefited only for a time. If, by contrast, we introduce them to the Dharma, so that they come to understand the painful reality of samsara and go on to practise, for example, the meditation on Chenrezig, we will have succeeded in helping them for their future lives as well. Again and again, we must work for the benefit of our parent sentient beings. Wanting happiness for themselves—alas, they wander in the different states of samsara. We are wandering in samsara like them and for the same reason. Therefore now, at this very moment, we should make a strong resolution to repay their kindness and work to dispel their suffering.

Beings are tormented by suffering. There is the extreme heat and cold of the hells and hunger and thirst in the realms of famished spirits. Animals suffer from being enslaved, while human beings are tortured by birth, disease, old age and death. The demigods are constantly fighting, and the gods themselves suffer when they must leave their heavenly abodes.

All suffering is the result of evil actions, while virtuous deeds are the cause of happiness and pleasure. The seeds of negativities left in the *alaya* are like promissory notes made out to a rich person when money is borrowed from him. When this person shows the promissory note, even after many years, there is no way that the debtor can avoid having to repay the loan. It is the same when we accumulate positive and negative actions: the results may not appear immediately, as when we have been cut by a knife; nevertheless, the effects of every one of our actions must be exhausted, either through purifying and confess-

ing them or through the experience of their consequences.
They do not simply disappear with the passage of time.
This is what is meant by the two Truths of Suffering and
the Origin of Suffering. 'Suffering' is the harm we actually
experience: the heat and cold of the hells, the hunger and
thirst of the realms of famished spirits, and so on. 'Origin'
is the seed of suffering—the promissory note to the
banker—which will afflict us in the future, not right
away.

We should decide to take upon ourselves the suffering
and the causes of suffering of all sentient beings (who
have all in previous existences been our mothers), and at
the same time to give away to them whatever causes of
happiness that we have. And if it happens that, as we
meditate upon their sufferings entering our hearts, we
begin to suffer ourselves, we should think with joy that
this is all for our mothers' sake. Giving away our own
happiness and positive deeds for their benefit, we should
ignore our own welfare for their sake, to the extent that
we are ready to give up even our lives for them. We must
try to provide a situation in which our mother sentient
beings might have happiness here and now, and circumstances suitable for them to practise the Dharma. We
should pray for them to be enlightened swiftly and take
delight in whatever progress they might make.

If we think continually in this way about our own
parents, we will eventually be able to care for them more
than for ourselves and likewise with regard to our brothers, sisters, friends and lovers. Then we should enlarge
our outlook to include everyone in our city, then in the
whole country. When we get used to that, we can try to
encompass all beings. If we do this gradually, our attitude
will increase in scope, our feelings will grow stable and
constant, and our love become ever more intense. Starting
thus with our mother and father, we should finally focus

on all sentient beings, who for countless lives have cared for us just like our present parents. We should feel a deep gratitude towards them. Knowing that all these parent-beings endure every kind of suffering in samsara, we should nourish one thought with fierce compassion: 'If only I could free them from this pain.'

To recapitulate: with an attitude of strong compassion, we imagine that the suffering of all beings dissolves into us, and in return we give our body, wealth and positive actions of the past, present and future. And if we see that beings are happy and their positive actions multiply, we should rejoice again and again.

The thought of exchanging happiness and suffering will come easily to us if we follow the pith instruction in the following root verse:

Mount them both upon your breath.

Visualize in front of you the person you dislike most. As you exhale, all your happiness, positive actions and wealth leave you like mist pushed by the wind. They dissolve into your enemy, who is thereby freed from suffering and filled with joy, becoming as happy as if he had been born in the Pure Land of Dewachen.[15] As you inhale, all his sufferings, negative actions and obscurations sink into you like dust on wind. Imagining that his sufferings actually fall upon you, feel their weight as though you were carrying a load. This will become easier with practice. By meditating in this way for a long time, over months and years, you will grow accustomed to it and your experience will develop as it should.

In the past one of Khenchen Tashi Oser's disciples lived as a hermit in the mountains. When a servant of his family died, he prayed for him, and one night dreamt that the servant had been reborn in one of the hot hells. When he awoke, the hermit went straight to Khenchen Tashi

Oser to whom he recounted the dream, requesting him to think of the deceased servant and to pray for him.

Khenchen Tashi Oser replied, 'I will think of him, but you should also practise the visualization of sending happiness and taking suffering. If you do it again and again, the person whom you have told me about will be liberated from the hell realms.'

So the ascetic returned to his cave and practised the visualization persistently. After seven days he found that he was covered with blisters. Thinking it was a sign, he went back to see Khenchen Tashi Oser.

'You told me to do the practice of giving and taking,' he said to his Teacher, 'and now it is as if my body has been burned by fire. I am covered with blisters.'

'It is just a sign,' said Khenchen Tashi Oser. 'Your former servant is now liberated from hell, and it shows also that you are able to give happiness and take suffering.'

If we are to get real benefit from this practice, we should continue until signs like these arise.

When the disciples of Adzom Drugpa[16] practised giving and taking, or *tonglen*, as it is called in Tibetan, they would do so thinking especially of people who had committed many heavy, negative actions. And it often happened that if they had previously gained some experience in meditation, their understanding would become clouded and they would feel that their obscurations had increased. Should signs like this occur, however, they are not to be taken as indications that future suffering is in store for us. Throughout his life, Geshe Karak Gomchung[17] prayed, 'May I be reborn in hell in place of those who have accumulated sinful actions.' He would repeat this prayer day and night. But just before he passed away he said: 'My prayers have not been fulfilled! For it seems that I am going to Dewachen; wherever I look, I see gardens full of flowers and a rain of blossom. Though I have prayed that all beings might go to Dewachen and that I myself might go to hell instead of them, in fact it seems that I am not going.' Such are the results of *tonglen*.

Relative Bodhichitta in post-meditation

Three objects, three poisons and three roots of virtue.

For objects that please us and for people that we love, for example our parents and relatives, we experience attachment. But when confronted by uncomfortable situations, when for example we see enemies or people we dislike, we experience aversion. When we see people who are neither close friends nor enemies, we feel indifferent. In pleasant situations, we feel attachment; in unpleasant situations, anger; in indifferent situations, ignorance.

Many people, like myself, are infected by the three poisons! Therefore we should pray, 'May the obscurations of all beings, arising through these three poisons, come upon me as a load to bear. May all beings live virtuously, performing positive actions, and be free from the three poisons of attachment, anger and ignorance.' We will be greatly benefited if we constantly train ourselves in thinking like this.

In all your actions, train yourself with maxims.

An example of these maxims would be: 'May the evil deeds of others ripen as my suffering; may all my virtuous acts bear fruit as others' happiness.' This is what the Kadampa masters always used to recite. It is good to repeat such verses in the post-meditation period. Moreover, praying like this will be even more beneficial before a precious object like the Jowo Rinpoche[18] in Lhasa or in

the presence of the Lama. If we do so, Bodhichitta is sure
to grow in us and therefore we should devote much time
and energy to this practice.

Begin the training sequence with yourself.

We should think like this: 'May all the torments des-
tined for me in the future, the heat and cold of the hells
and the hunger and thirst of the famished spirits, come to
me now. And may all the karma, obscuration and defile-
ment causing beings to fall into an infernal destiny sink
into my heart so that I myself might go to hell instead of
them. May the suffering of others, the fruit, as the teachings say, of their desire and ignorance, come to me.' We
should train ourselves like this again and again until we
have such signs as that of Maitriyogin, who was wound-
ed in the place where the stone had hit the dog.

Bodhichitta, the mind of enlightenment, is the heart of
all the practices of the Sutra and Mantrayana, and it is
easy to implement. If one has it, everything is complete,
and nothing is complete without it. At this present time,
you are receiving many teachings on mind-training from
different teachers. Keep them in your hearts! When they
are translated, I hope that you will understand and remember them. For this is indeed the Dharma.

III

CARRYING DIFFICULT SITUATIONS
ONTO THE PATH OF ENLIGHTENMENT

BODHICHITTA may be considered under two further headings: Bodhichitta in intention and Bodhichitta in action. Beginning with the former we find that it likewise has two aspects according as it is related to the relative, or to the absolute, truth.

> *When all the world is filled with evils,*
> *Place all setbacks on the path of liberation.*

If we have instructions on how to carry obstacles onto the path, then no matter how many difficulties and conflicting situations come upon us, they will simply clarify our practice and have no power to hinder us on the path. If, however, we do not have such instructions, then difficulties will be experienced as hindrances.

In these degenerate times, as far as the outer universe is concerned, the rains and snows do not come when they should, harvests are poor, the cattle are unhealthy and people and animals are riddled with disease. Because people spend their time in evil activities, because they are jealous and constantly wish misfortune on one another, many countries are at variance and in desperate circumstances. We are in the era when even the teachings of religion are perverted so that famine, disease and war are

rife. But, when a forest is on fire, a gale will only make it
bigger, it certainly will not blow it out. Likewise, for a
Bodhisattva who has received instruction, all such cata-
strophic situations may be profitably taken onto the path.

Guru Padmasambhava has said, 'Pray to me, you beings of degenerate times, who have not the fortune to
meet with the Buddhas and Bodhisattvas of the ten direc-
tions. My compassion will be swift to shield you.' As an
illustration of this, think of Tibet, a place where Buddha
Shakyamuni[19] never went. When the abbot Shantarakshita,[20] Vajrapani[21] in person, went there to teach the
Buddhadharma, his work was hindered by ferocious and
terrible evil spirits. Because of that inauspicious circumstance, Guru Rinpoche was invited. He came, and with
the weapons of voidness and compassion subdued all the
negative forces, blessing the entire country as a Buddhafield of Chenrezig, causing the tradition of the Mantrayana to rise and shine like the sun. This is an example of
Bodhisattva activity.

We might however think that in order to carry everything onto the path to enlightenment, we need to be
someone like Guru Rinpoche, with high realization and
miraculous power, qualities which, alas, we do not have.
We should not discourage ourselves with thoughts of
that kind! By following these instructions, we will be able
to make use of every difficult situation in our spiritual
training.

Bodhichitta in intention related to the relative truth

All suffering comes through not recognising ego-clinging
as our enemy. When we are hit by a stick or a stone, it
hurts; when someone calls us a thief or a liar, we become
angry. Why is this? It is because we feel great esteem and
attachment for what we think of as our *selves*, and we
think '*I* am being attacked.' Clinging to the 'I' is the real

obstacle to the attainment of liberation and enlightenment. What we call obstacle-makers or evil influences, such as ghosts, gods, and so on, are not at all entities outside us. It is from within that the trouble comes. It is due to our fixation on 'I,' that we think: 'I am so unhappy, I can't get anything to eat, I have no clothes, lots of people are against me and I don't have any friends.' It is thoughts like these that keep us so busy—and all so uselessly! This is the reason why we are not on the path to liberation and Buddhahood. Throughout the entire succession of our lives, from beginningless time until the present, we have been taking birth in one or other of the six realms. How long we have been labouring in the three worlds of samsara, slaves to our ego-clinging! This is why we cannot escape. When a man has borrowed a lot of money, he will never have a moment's peace until he has repaid his debt. So it is with all the work that our ego-clinging has given us to do; it has left negative imprints on the alaya similar to promissory notes. When our karma fructifies and 'payment' is demanded, we have no chance for happiness and enjoyment. All this is because, as it says in the teachings, we do not recognize ego-clinging as our real enemy.

It is also because we do not recognise the great kindness of beings. It was said by Buddha Shakyamuni that to work for beings with kindness and compassion, and to make offerings to the Buddhas are of equal value for the attainment of enlightenment. Therefore to be generous to others, to free them from suffering and set them on the path of liberation is as good as making offerings to the Buddhas. We may think that it is better to give to a temple, or place offerings before an image of the Buddha. In fact, because the Buddhas are completely free from self cherishing, the more we can help beings, the happier they are. When the hordes of demons tried to obstruct the Buddha

as he was on the point of attaining enlightenment, sending their armies and hurling their weapons, he meditated
on kindness towards them, whereupon his great love
overwhelmed their hatred, turning their weapons into
flowers, and their curses and war cries into praises and
mantras. Other beings are in fact the best occasions for
the accumulation of merit.

This is why the Bodhisattvas in Dewachen (a pure
Buddhafield where there are no afflicted beings and no
objects of hatred, pride and envy) pray to be reborn in this
sorrowing world of ours. For, as the sutras say, they want
to be in a place where beings think only of accumulating
possessions and satisfying those close to them, where
they are therefore overwhelmed by defilements and so
are supports for the mind training and practice of
Bodhichitta. The immediate causes for the attainment of
Buddhahood are other beings; we should be truly grateful to them.

Lay the blame for everything on one.

All suffering, all sickness, possession by spirits, loss of
wealth, involvements with the law and so on, are without
exception the result of clinging to the 'I.' That is indeed
where we should lay the blame for all our mishaps. All
the suffering that comes to us arises simply through our
holding on to our ego. We should not blame anything on
others. Even if some enemy were to come and cut our
heads off or beat us with a stick, all he does is to provide
the momentary circumstance of injury. The real cause of
our being harmed is our self-clinging and is not the work
of our enemy. As it is said:

> All the harm with which this world is rife,
> All the fear and suffering that there is:
> Clinging to the 'I' has caused it!
> What am I to do with this great demon?

When people believe that their house is haunted or that a particular object is cursed, they think that they have to have it exorcized. Ordinary people are often like that, aren't they? But ghosts, devils and so on are only external enemies; they cannot really harm us. But as soon as the inner ghost of ego-clinging appears—that is when the real trouble starts.

A basis for ego-clinging has never at any time existed. We cling to our 'I,' even when in fact there is nothing to cling to. We cling to it and cherish it. For its sake we bring harm to others, accumulating many negative actions, only to endure much suffering in samsara, in the lower realms, later on.

It says in the *Bodhicharyavatara*:

> O you my mind, for countless ages past,
> Have sought the welfare of yourself;
> Oh the weariness it brought upon you!
> And all you got was sorrow in return.

It is not possible to point to a moment and say, 'This was when I started in samsara; this is how long I have been here.' Without the boundless knowledge of a Buddha, it is impossible to calculate such an immense period of time.

Because we are sunk in the delusion of ego-clinging, we think in terms of 'my body, my mind, my name.' We think we own them and take care of them. Anything that does them harm, we will attack. Anything that helps them, we will become attached to. All the calamities and loss that come from this are therefore said to be the work of ego-clinging and since this is the source of suffering, we can see that it is indeed our enemy. Our minds which cling to the illusion of self, have brought forth misery in samsara from beginningless time. How does this come about? When we come across someone richer, more

learned or with a better situation than ourselves, we think
that they are showing off, and we are determined to do
better. We are jealous, and want to cut them down to size.
When those less fortunate than ourselves ask for help, we
think, 'What's the point of helping a beggar like this? He
will never be able to repay me. I just can't be bothered
with him.' When we come across someone of equal status
who has some wealth, we also want some. If they have
fame we also want to be famous. If they have a good
situation, we want a good situation too. We always want
to compete. This is why we are not free from samsara: it
is this that creates the sufferings and harm which we
imagine to be inflicted on us by spirits and other human
beings.

Once when he was plagued by gods and demons,
Milarepa said to them: 'If you must eat my body, eat it! If
you want to drink my blood, drink it! Take my life and
breath immediately, and go!' As soon as he relinquished
all concern for himself, all difficulties dissolved and the
obstacle-makers paid him homage.

That is why the author of the *Bodhicharyavatara* says to
the ego:

> A hundred harms you've done me
> Wandering in cycles of existence;
> Now your malice I remember
> And will crush your selfish schemes!

The degree of self-clinging that we have is the measure
of the harms we suffer. In this world, if a person has been
seriously wronged by one of his fellows, he would think,
'I am the victim of that man's terrible crimes, I must fight
back. He ought to be put to death, or at least the author-
ities should put him in prison; he should be made to pay
to his last penny.' And if the injured man succeeds in
these intentions, he would be considered a fine, upstand-

ing, courageous person. But it is only if we really have the wish to put an end to the ego-clinging which has brought us pain and loss from beginningless time—it is only then, that we will be on the path to enlightenment.

And so, when attachment for the 'I' appears—and it is after all only a thought within our minds—we should try to investigate. Is this ego a substance, a thing? Is it inside or outside? When we think that someone has done something to hurt us and anger arises, we should ask ourselves whether the anger is part of the enemy's makeup or whether it is in ourselves. Likewise with attachment to friends: is our longing an attribute of the friend, or is it in ourselves? And if there are such things as anger or attachment, do they have shape or colour, are they male, female or neither? For if they exist, they ought to have characteristics. The fact is, however, that even if we persevere in our search, we will never find anything. If we do not find anything, how is it that we keep on clinging? All the trouble that we have had to endure until now has been caused by something that has never existed! Therefore, whenever the ego-clinging arises we must rid ourselves of it immediately and we should do everything within our power to prevent it from arising again. As Shantideva says in the *Bodhicharyavatara*:

> That time when you could beat me down
> Is in the past, it's no more here.
> Now I see you! Where will you escape?
> I will crush your haughty insolence!

'In this short lifetime,' Geshe Shawopa used to say, 'we should subdue this demon as much as possible.' Just as one would go to lamas for initiations and rituals to exorcize a haunted house, in the same way, to drive away this demon of ego-clinging, we should meditate on Bodhichitta and try to establish ourselves in the view of

emptiness. We should fully understand, as Geshe Shawopa would say, that all the experiences we undergo are
the fruit of good or evil actions that we have done to
others in the past. He had the habit of giving worldly
names to selfish actions, and religious names to actions
done for others. Then there was Geshe Ben who, when a
positive thought occurred to him, would praise it highly,
and when a negative thought arose, would apply the
antidote at once and beat it off.

The only way to guard the door of the mind is with the
spear of the antidote. No other way exists. When the
enemy is strong, we too have to be on the alert. When the
enemy is mild we can loosen up a little bit as well. For
example when there is trouble in a kingdom, the body-
guards will protect the king constantly, neither sleeping
at night nor relaxing by day. Likewise, in order to drive
away the mischief-maker of our ego-clinging, we should
apply the antidote of emptiness as soon as it appears. This
is what Geshe Shawopa used to call 'the ritual of exorcism.'

Let us regard ego-clinging therefore as our enemy.
When it exists no longer, it will be impossible for us not
to care for others more than we do for ourselves. As this
feeling arises, let us

Reflect upon the kindness of all beings

for they have been our parents and have shown us much
goodness countless times in the past. Of the thousand
Buddhas of this age, it is said that Buddha Shakyamuni
was the one who had the greatest aspirations. For when
the others conceived the wish to be enlightened for the
sake of beings, they aspired to Buddhafields, longevity,
great congregations of Shravakas etc. But the Buddha
Shakyamuni prayed to be reborn in degenerate times,
when it would be difficult to teach beings afflicted by

disease, famine and war. He took birth in this realm knowingly, praying that whoever heard his name or his teachings might straight away be set upon the path of liberation. That is why, with his armour-like aspirations and endeavour, the Buddha Shakyamuni is without equal and is praised as a white lotus among the thousand Buddhas of this fortunate kalpa.

We should be thankful to all beings, for enlightenment depends on them, and have as much love and compassion towards our enemies as we have towards our friends. This is the most important thing, because love and compassion for parents, husbands, wives, brothers and sisters arises naturally by itself. It is said in the *Bodhicharyavatara*:

> The state of Buddhahood depends
> On beings and the Buddhas equally.
> By what tradition is it then that
> Buddhas, but not beings, are alone revered?

For example, if we find an image of the Buddha, or even a single word or page of the scriptures, in a low and dirty place, we respectfully pick them up and place them somewhere clean and high. When we see beings, we should respect them in the same way. Whenever he saw a dog lying in the street, Dromtönpa[22] would never step over it, but, reflecting that the animal also had the potential for Buddhahood, would circumambulate it. Thus towards Buddhas and beings, we should have an equal reverence. In whichever sadhana we perform, immediately after taking refuge, we generate the attitude of Bodhichitta, and from that moment on, other beings become the support for our practice. We may thus appreciate their significance. For the one who wishes to attain enlightenment, the Buddhas and sentient beings have an equal kindness. With regard to those to whom we owe so much, we should meditate very strongly: generating an intense love, wishing them every happiness, and having great compassion, wanting them to be free from suffering.

If people are sick, we should wish to take their suffering upon ourselves. When we meet a beggar, we should be generous to him. In this way, we shoulder the sufferings of others and send them all our happiness, fame, long life, power etc.—whatever we have.

Especially, if we are the victims of harm inflicted by human or non human beings, we should not think, 'This being is harming me, therefore I will make him and his descendants pay.' No, we must not bear grudges. Instead we should think to ourselves: 'This evil-doer has for countless lives been my mother—my mother who, not caring for all the suffering she had to undergo for my sake, not listening to all the bad things people might say, took care of me and endured much suffering in samsara. For my sake, this being has accumulated many negative actions. Yet, in my delusion, I do not recognize him as a relation from the past. The harm which I suffer at the hands of others is provoked by my bad karma. Because of *my* past negative actions, my enemy has hurt me and accumulated negative karma, which he in future will have to expiate. Because of *me*, this person has endured suffering in the past and will certainly do so in the future.' Thus we should try to be very loving towards such beings, thinking, 'Until now I have only harmed others. Henceforward, I will free them from all their ills and be of help to them.' In this way, we should perform the practice of taking and giving very intensely.

If bitten by a dog or attacked by someone, instead of reacting angrily, we should try to help our aggressor as much as possible. And even if we cannot help, we must not give up the wish to do so. When in the presence of sick people, whom we cannot cure, we can visualize the Medicine Buddha above their heads and pray that they will be freed from their disease. If we do so, this will automatically be of benefit to them. Moreover, we should act with the deepest conviction and pray that the harmful beings which were the cause of the sickness might also be free from suffering and quickly attain enlightenment. We should decide that from now on, whatever virtuous actions we perform, the riches or longevity we gain, even Buddhahood itself—all these will be exclusively for the benefit of others. Whatever good might come to us, we will give it all away. What does it matter, then, if we attain enlightenment or not, if our lives are long or short, if we are rich or poor. None of this matters!

Even if we have the impression that we are under attack from evil spirits, we should think: 'Because for countless lives I myself have fed upon your flesh and blood, it is natural that I should now repay you in kind. Therefore I will give you everything.' And we imagine that we lay our bodies open before them, as when an animal is butchered. As it is said in the practice of *chöd*:

> Those come from afar, let them eat it raw!
> Those who are close by, let them eat it cooked!
> Grind my bones and eat your fill!
> Whatever you can carry, take away!
> Consume whatever you are able!

Saying this aloud, we let go of all clinging to ourselves. We imagine that when the harmful spirits have satisfied their hunger, their bodies are filled with a bliss free from negative emotions, and that the experience of the two Bodhichittas arises in them. This is how we should offer our bodies to what are thought to be the ghosts and demons who feed on flesh and blood. We should imagine that with this offering of our bodies, they are totally satisfied and have no further intention to kill or harm others, that they are content and pleased with all they have received.

In short, all suffering comes from the enemy of our own ego-clinging; all benefit derives from other beings, who are therefore like friends and relatives. We should try to help them as much as possible. As Langri Tangpa Dorje Gyaltsen[23] said, 'Of all the profound teachings I have read, this only have I understood: that all harm and sorrow are my own doing and all benefit and qualities are thanks to others. Therefore all my gain I give to others; all loss I take upon myself.' He perceived this as the sole meaning of all the texts that he had studied, meditating upon it throughout his life.

Bodhichitta in intention related to the absolute truth

> *Voidness is the unsurpassed protection;*
> *Thereby illusory appearance is seen as the four*
>   *kayas.*

Sufferings related to the universe and its inhabitants are the result of false perceptions, the nature of which it is important to understand. Emotions, such as attachment, anger and ignorance are all creations of the mind. We think, for instance, of our body as a precious possession of which we must take special care, protecting it from illness and every kind of mishap. We get into this habit of thinking and, as a consequence, begin to suffer mentally as well as physically. This is an example of perception which, since it is devoid of any basis in reality, is called deluded; it depends upon the belief in the existence of something which does not exist at all. It is just as when we dream and think that we are being burned or drowned, only to discover, when we wake up, that nothing has happened.

From the point of view of absolute truth, phenomena have no actual entity. What we think of as 'I,' 'my body,' 'my mind,' 'my name,' have no real existence. Other beings have no real existence either, whether they be dangerous enemies or loving parents. In the same way, the five poisons are by nature empty. Bearing this fact in mind, we should watch from where these poisons, these negative emotions arise, what does the agent of these arisings look like, and what do the emotions themselves look like? If we analyse, we shall find nothing. This absence is the unborn Dharmakaya.

Although everything is by nature empty, this emptiness is not the mere vacuity of empty space or an empty vessel. Happiness, sufferings, all sorts of feelings and perceptions appear endlessly like reflected images in the mind. This reflection-like appearance of phenomena is called the Nirmanakaya.

A grain not planted in the soil will never give a fruit, likewise that which is unborn will never cease to be. To be beyond origination is to be beyond cessation also. This aspect of unceasingness is what should be understood as the Sambhogakaya.

If there is neither birth, in the past, nor cessation, in the future, there cannot be something which endures in the present; for an existence necessarily implies a beginning and an end. For example, though it might be thought that, while we are alive, the mind resides in the body, in fact there is no residing and no one who resides; there is no existence and nothing that exists. Even if one were to separate the skin, the flesh, the muscles and the blood, of the body, where would the mind be found? Is it in the flesh or in the bone, etc? Nothing will be found, for the mind itself is void. The fact that the mind is by nature empty, that it is nevertheless the place where phenomena appear, and that it is beyond origination and is therefore unceasing—this inseparable union of the three kayas is called the Svabhavikakaya.

If deluded perceptions are understood in terms of the four kayas, it follows that in that which is termed deluded, there is nothing impure, nothing to rid ourselves of. Neither is there something else, pure and undeluded, which we should try to adopt. For, indeed, when illusion dissolves, undeluded wisdom is simply present, where it always has been. When gold is in the ground, for example, it is blemished and stained; but the nature of gold as such is not susceptible to change. When it is purified by chemicals or refined by a goldsmith, its real character increasingly shines forth. In the same way, if we subject the deluded mind to analysis, and reach the conclusion that it is free from birth, cessation and abiding existence, we will discover, then and there, a wisdom which is undeluded. Furthermore, the deluded mind, being itself illusory, is unstable and fluctuates, like experiences in a dream, whereas the true and undeluded nature of phenomena, the Buddha-nature or Tathagatagarbha, has been present from unoriginated time. It is exactly the same in ourselves as it is in the Buddhas. It is thanks to it that the Buddhas are able to bring help to beings; it is thanks to it, too, that beings may attain enlightenment. There is no other introduction to the four kayas than this understanding of the true nature of illusory perception.

We should be thankful, therefore, to our enemies for stimulating our experience of relative and absolute Bodhichitta. It was the same, for example, with Milarepa. When his aunt and uncle turned against him and his mother, reducing them to beggary, he was eventually spurred into going to seek the help of Marpa.[24] He then practised with such diligence that within his very lifetime he attained unsurpassable accomplishment so that his fame filled both the noble land of India and Tibet, the

Land of Snow. All this came to pass because of the actions of criminals. Therefore we should be grateful for the stimulus that they provide. For indeed, as long as we are unable to make use of the antidote, as described above, and negative emotions are at work in us without our noticing, it is through the activity of those who do us harm that we are made aware of them. Consequently it is as if they were emanations of our Teacher and the Buddhas. Suppose we are afflicted by a deadly disease, or even if we are only unwell, we should think, 'If I were not sick, I should be lost in the futility of trying to make this life pleasant, giving no thought to Dharma. But because I am suffering, I think of death, turn to the teachings and reflect upon them. All this is the activity of my Teacher and the Three Jewels.' We all know that Bodhichitta begins to develop in us when we have met with a Teacher and received his teachings. If, with the seed of Bodhichitta once planted in our hearts, we continue to practise, evildoers and the troubles they cause, indeed suffering in general, will all conspire to make our Bodhichitta grow. There is therefore no difference between our enemies and our Teachers. Knowing that suffering brings about the growth of the two Bodhichittas, we must take advantage of it.

When Shantarakshita came to Tibet and began to teach, his work was hindered by evil forces and local spirits too. Heavy storms occurred which even washed away the Red Hill Palace. Because of these disastrous circumstances, Shantarakshita and the king invited Guru Padmasambhava, who came and caused the Buddhadharma to shine like the sun. If those negative forces had not arisen, perhaps the precious Guru would never have been invited to Tibet. Likewise, if the Buddha had not had to contend with the demons, he might never have attained enlightenment. Thus we should meditate constantly, always putting difficult situations to good use.

Bodhichitta in action

The best of methods is to have four practices.

The practices referred to here are accumulation, purification, offerings to evil forces and offerings to the Dharma Protectors.

Accumulation. When we are in pain, we naturally wish that we were not suffering. If therefore we do not want to suffer and want to be well, we should recite the name of the Medicine Buddha and make offerings to the Buddhas and Bodhisattvas—all of which is a cause of health and happiness. We should consequently exert ourselves in making offerings to the Lama and the Three Jewels, paying homage to the monastic order, and giving tormas to the spirits.

We should take refuge and generate Bodhichitta. Then we should offer a mandala to the Teacher and the Three Jewels praying as follows: 'If it is better for me to be sick, I pray that you will send me sickness to purify the stains and obscurations of my sinful karma. But if my being cured means that I will accomplish the Dharma, that physically and mentally I will practise virtue and make progress on the path, then I pray that you will bless me with health. But if it is better for me to die so as to be reborn in a pure Buddhafield, then I pray you, send me the blessing of death.' It is very important to pray frequently like this, for thereby we will free ourselves of hope and fear.

Purification. When we suffer, we should regard our discomfort as a sign reminding us that the way to avoid even minor pains is to abandon all negative actions. In the purification of negativities, there are four powers to be considered.

The first is the power of revulsion, a strong regret for all evil actions committed in the past, similar to the regret we might feel after swallowing poison. It is futile to confess faults without regret, and the power of revulsion is simply to be sick of one's negative actions. The second power is the decision to improve. In the past, we have failed to recognise the evil of negative actions; but from now on, even at the cost of our lives, we resolve to refrain from negativity. The third power is that of the support. Since it is impossible to make confession without having someone to confess to, we take as our object the Three Jewels, whose Body, Speech and Mind are ever free from evil actions, and who are utterly without partiality. When we have taken refuge in them, the best way to purify ourselves is to generate Bodhichitta in their presence. Just as it is said that all forests will be consumed in an instant by the fires at the end of the kalpa, likewise all negative actions are completely purified by the generation of Bodhichitta. The fourth power is the power of the anti-dote. One such antidote is the meditation on emptiness, for even negative actions are by nature empty and have no substantial existence as independent entities. As another antidote, it is said that the mere recollection of the mantra of Chenrezig can bring about enlightenment. The six syllables of the Mani correspond to Chenrezig's accomplishment of the six transcendent perfections and are manifestations of them. By hearing the mantra, beings are liberated from samsara; by thinking of the mantra, they accomplish these perfections. The benefit of the Mani is so vast that if the earth could be used as paper, the trees as pens and the oceans as ink, and if the Buddhas themselves were to discourse upon it, there would be no end to the description of its qualities. Practices such as medi-

tation on emptiness or the recitation of the Mani consti-
tute the power of applying the antidote of wholesome
conduct. The Buddha said in the White Lotus of Compassion Sutra that if someone were to practise properly the
recitation of the six syllables, even the parasites living in
his body would be reborn in Chenrezig's Buddhafield.

Confession is practised correctly when these four powers are all present. As it is said by the Kadampa Masters,
negative actions have but one good quality: they may be
purified through confession.

Offerings to evil forces. When offering tormas to evil
spirits, we should say with great conviction, 'When you
do me harm, I practise patience and therefore you are
helping me to train in Bodhichitta. I am grateful. Use your
great power to cause the sufferings of all beings to come
to me.' If however we lack such courage, we can simply
offer them tormas with feelings of love and compassion
and say: 'I shall try to do you good both now and in the
future; do not hinder me in accomplishing the Dharma.'

Offerings to the Dharma Protectors. When we offer tormas to the Protectors, Mahakala, Pelden Lhamo and the
like, we request their help in our meditation and practice
of Bodhichitta so as to be able to care for all beings in the
same way as we do for our parents or our children. Let
us pray to be completely free from anger towards our
enemies and to overcome the delusion of ego-clinging.
Let us ask them to remove from our path all causes of
conflict and to bring about favourable circumstances.

> To bring the unexpected to the path,
> Begin to train immediately.

There is no certainty that we will not fall victim to
disease, evil forces and so on. If we are afflicted by serious
illness, we should think, 'There are countless beings in

this world suffering in the same way as I.' In this way we should generate strong feelings of compassion. If, for example, we are struck by heart disease, we should think, 'Wherever space pervades, there are beings suffering like this,' and imagine that all their illnesses are concentrated in our own hearts.

If we are struck by evil forces, we should think, 'By making me suffer, these evil beings are helping me to practise Bodhichitta; they are of great importance for my progress on the path, and rather than being expelled, they should be thanked.' We should be as grateful to them as we are towards our Teachers.

Again, if we see others in trouble, although we cannot immediately take their suffering upon ourselves, we should make the wish to be able to relieve them from their misfortunes. Prayers like this will bear fruit eventually. Again, if others have very strong afflictive emotions, we should think, 'May all their emotions be concentrated in me.' With fervent conviction, we should persist in thinking like this until we have some sign or feeling that we have been able to take upon ourselves the suffering and emotions of others. This might take the form of an increase in our own emotions or of the actual experience of the suffering and pain of others.

This is how to bring hardships onto the path in order to free ourselves from hopes and fears—hopes, for instance, that we will not get ill, or fears that we might do so. They will thus be pacified in the equal taste of happiness and suffering. Eventually, through the power of Bodhichitta, we will reach the point where we are free even from the hope of accomplishing Bodhichitta and the fear of not doing so. Therefore we should have love for our enemies and try as much as possible to avoid getting angry with them, or harbouring any negative thoughts towards them. We should also try as much as possible to overcome our biased attachment to family and relatives. If you bind a crooked tree to a large wooden stake, it will eventually grow straight. Up to now, our minds have always been crooked, thinking how we might trick and mislead people, but this practice, as Geshe Langri Tangpa said, will make our minds straight and true.

IV

AN EXPLANATION OF THE PRACTICE
AS A WAY OF LIFE

The pith instructions briefly summarized:
Put the five strengths into practice.

IF we possess these five strengths, Bodhichitta will arise in us. They are as follows: the power of resolution, the power of familiarization, the power of the positive seed, the power of revulsion and the power of aspiration.

The power of resolution. This is, for example, the taking of a firm decision that, for this month, this year, until we die or until we attain enlightenment, we will not abandon Bodhichitta; even though hurt or injured by others, we will not give way to anger. And this strong resolution should be reinforced again and again.

The power of familiarization. In the beginning, meditation is difficult but it becomes easier if we persevere in it. For as the saying goes, 'There is nothing that one cannot get used to.'

Once upon a time, there was a very miserly person unable to give anything away. He went to see the Buddha.

'It is impossible for me to be generous,' he said, 'what shall I do?'

'Imagine,' the Buddha replied, 'that your right hand is yourself and your left hand a poor unhappy person. Give from your right hand to your left some old food, which you don't like or need. Try hard to get used to this. Do it until you are no longer miserly.'

The man began the practice, but he was so tight-fisted that at first he could give away only a few left-overs or food he did not like. Gradually, however, he acquired the habit so that the day arrived when he did not feel so niggardly. Thereupon, he went to see the Buddha and reported, 'Now when I give food from my right hand to my left, I don't feel so miserly.' Buddha replied, 'Now, with your right hand, which you take to be yourself, give some gold, silk or fine clothes to your left hand, which you imagine to be a beggar. Try to see if you can give open-handedly, without avarice.' The man tried and when he got used to it he went again to see the Buddha. 'Now, you can be a benefactor,' the Buddha said, 'you are free from attachment; you can give away food and clothing to those who lack them.'

Freed from his miserliness, the man thus came to help many beggars and poor people. He gradually practised and in the end his generosity was steady, without any wavering. He understood that there is no point in being parsimonious or attached to riches. He became a monk and attained the level of an arhat. Through persistent practice one may likewise become accomplished in the two Bodhichittas.

The power of positive seeds. This is, in fact, the accumulation of merit. Going to temples and monasteries, performing prostrations and devotions before sacred objects, we should pray, 'May I be able to cultivate the two types of Bodhichitta. May I be peaceful and without anger towards those who do me harm. May I be free from

one-sided attachment for friends and relatives.' By repeatedly praying in this way, and through the power of
the Buddhas and Bodhisattvas, we will be able to accomplish these qualities.

The power of revulsion. Through careful thought it is
possible to see that all the suffering and afflictive emo-
tional states experienced in life are the results of the
devastating flood of ego-clinging. Ego-clinging is the
cause of every ill. Therefore when it arises, even if only
for an instant, we should apply the antidote, like the
doctor who gives us healing medicine when we are sick.
As the saying goes, 'Hit the pig on the nose; clean the
lamp while it is still warm.' When an angry pig rears up
at us, if we hit it on the nose with a stick, it will immediately turn round and run away, unable to bear the pain.
If we clean the butter-lamp while it is still warm, the job
is very easily done. In the same way, if we apply the
antidote before our ego-clinging has gathered strength,
we shall not fall under its influence.

The power of aspiration. Whenever we have completed
some positive action we should pray, 'From now on until
I attain enlightenment, may I never abandon the two
Bodhichittas. Whatever conflicts I may encounter, may I
be able to use them as steps along the path.' Praying in
this way, we should make offerings to the Teacher, the
Three Jewels and the Dharma Protectors, asking for their
assistance.

It is said of these five powers that they are the whole
of the teachings condensed into a single syllable *HUNG.*
The meaning of this is that all the profound and elaborate instructions of the Mind Training are contained
within the five powers. Therefore we should practise
them fervently, as did the Buddha himself when once,

in a previous life, he was the royal hermit Kshantivadin, the Forbearing.

The story goes that he had withdrawn into the forest as an ascetic whereupon his younger brother had succeeded to the throne. One day the king, the younger brother, went on an expedition and at some point he took his rest and fell asleep. Meanwhile his queens, the ministers and attendants went off to see hermit Kshantivadin, whom they knew from before, and requested him to teach them. When the king awoke, he found that he was alone and, thinking that the queens, ministers and attendants had abandoned him, became very angry. He arose and searched and found them grouped around the hermit. Not realizing that the holy man was teaching the Dharma, the king thought that he was leading his queens and ministers astray and corrupting them.

'Who are you?' cried the king. For he had been very young when his brother had renounced the world and did not recognize him.

'I am hermit Kshantivadin,' replied his elder brother.

'Well,' said the king, 'let us see if you are worthy of such a name. Let me see how much you can bear.' So saying, he cut off the sage's right hand. 'Well, can you bear that?' he said.

'Yes, I can,' came the reply.

Cutting off the hermit's left hand, the king said, 'Are you still Kshantivadin, can you still bear that?'

'Yes,' he said.

Then the king struck off the hermit's head, saying, 'Can you still bear that?'

'Yes,' he said.

And so it was that he cut off the hermit's hands and head. But from his wounds, instead of blood, there flowed a white milky substance. The king calmed down, and thinking that this could not be an ordinary being, he asked his retinue who it was. 'It is your brother, Kshantivadin,' they told him, 'who in the past renounced the kingdom to go to the forest.' Thereupon, the king felt great remorse and began to weep. Now Kshantivadin was a Bodhisattva, and so, although his head had been cut off, he could still talk. He said: 'My hands and head you cut off as you asked your questions, therefore in the future, when I become a Buddha, may I be able to cut off your defilements as you question me.'

In fact Kshantivadin was later to become the Buddha Shakyamuni.

After the Buddha's enlightenment, the first five disciples (one of whom had been Kshantivadin's brother in a previous life) asked him: 'What is samsara?'

The Buddha said: 'Samsara is by nature suffering.'

Then they asked: 'Whence does suffering arise?'

Buddha said: 'Suffering arises from defiled emotions.'

Then they asked: 'How can we eradicate the cause of suffering?'

Buddha said: 'You must follow the path.'

Then they asked: 'What is the good of following the path?'

Buddha said: 'All karma and emotions come thereby to cessation.' And it was through this teaching that the five disciples attained arhatship. So, although the head of Kshantivadin was chopped off in anger, yet, through the power of his aspirations for enlightenment, he was able to transform that evil karmic connection into the positive cause of the king's becoming his disciple later on. We can see from this why the Dharma teaches the necessity of making prayers of aspiration.

We will now speak about the instructions for dying according to this Dharma tradition. For the practice of the transference of consciousness according to the teachings of the Mind Training , it is as the root verses say:

> *On how to die, the Mahayana teaches*
> *These five strengths. It matters how you act.*

These five strengths are the same as those just mentioned: positive seeds, aspiration, revulsion, resolution and familiarization.

The power of positive seeds. When we practitioners realize that we are about to die, that we are in the grip of a fatal disease, and that there is no way that we can prolong our lives, we should make an offering to our Teacher and the Three Jewels of all our possessions, giving them away wherever it is most beneficial and meritorious. We should deal with all our unfinished business and have no attachment or aversion for anyone or anything.

The power of aspiration. Making the seven branch offering to our Teacher and the Three Jewels, we should pray as follows: 'May I be free from fear in the bardo, and in all my future lives may I be blessed with the practice of the twofold Bodhichitta. May the Victorious Ones bless me, especially the master who has taught me the Bodhichitta practice, the Mind Training instructions.' We should pray like this again and again, confident that our Teacher will take care of us.

The power of revulsion. We should remember that ego-clinging has brought us sorrow in the past. Even now, the hope that we might continue to live, attachment to our bodies as something precious, worries as to the way in which our wealth will be used: all this might still occasion a lot of suffering. If even now we are unable to rid ourselves of such clinging, we will never have peace. We should let our bodies go like earth and stones, thinking that they are not worth holding on to. We are suffering just because of our attachment to them. Just look!—on the outside they are skin, inside they are filled with flesh, blood, bones and all sorts of disgusting substances. They are actually nothing but bags of dirt and there is no need to identify them as ourselves. Let them be burned; let the birds or dogs devour them! Reflecting in this way, we rid ourselves of self-cherishing.

The power of resolution. We should remind ourselves that when we have to pass through the bardo, by meditating on the precious Bodhichitta, we will in fact be meditating on the heart essence of all Buddhas and Bodhisattvas. It will be impossible for us to fall into the lower realms. By resolving to practise Bodhichitta constantly with strong determination, we guard ourselves from the terror of the bardo.

The power of familiarization. We should constantly be mulling over the techniques just described: how to practise the twofold Bodhichitta, how to exchange happiness for suffering, how to develop compassion towards those who are hostile. We must live in such a way that, through remembering the Mind Training constantly, we will be able to apply it when the time comes for us to die and we are in a lot of pain.

Now when the moment of death arrives, this is what you should do. Just as the Buddha did when he passed away, lie on your right side, rest your head on your right hand. Breathe in through your left nostril, blocking your right nostril with the little finger of your right hand. Meditate on love, wishing happiness for all beings, numerous as the sky is vast, and generate compassion with the desire to free them from every suffering. Using the support of your ingoing and outgoing breaths, imagine that you exhale all your happiness, comfort and wealth, sending them to all who suffer. And inhale all the diseases, evil, negative emotions and obscurations of other beings, taking them upon yourselves.

Afterwards, you should reflect that samsara and nirvana are themselves illusory, just like a dream or a wizard's magical display. Everything is devoid of self-existence. Everything is but the perception of the mind and where nothing exists, there is no cause for fear, here or in the bardo. Try to remain in that conviction, without any mental grasping.

An old lady and her daughter were once swept away by a river. The lady thought to herself, 'If only my daughter could be saved, I do not care if I drown!' The daughter thought, 'What does it matter if I die? Only let my mother be safe!' They were both killed, but, because their final intentions were those of such a powerful love, they were reborn in the realms of the gods. And so we should have loving thoughts like this all the time, and when we come to die, we should meditate alternately upon the two Bodhichittas.

There are many well-known and celebrated instructions on how to transfer the consciousness at the moment of death, but none are so sublime, amazing or wonderful as this.

V

STANDARDS OF PROFICIENCY IN THE MIND TRAINING

All Dharma has a single goal.

THE Buddha gave eighty-four thousand different teachings, all of them designed to subdue ego-clinging. This was the only reason why he set them forth. If they do not act as an antidote for our attachment to self, then all practice is in vain, as was the case with the Buddha's cousin Devadatta. He knew as many sutras as an elephant could carry on its back, but because he could not shake off his clinging to self, he went to hell in his next life.

The extent to which we have been able to overcome our self-attachment will show the degree to which we have used the Dharma properly. So let us try very hard.

Rely upon the better of two witnesses.

If we have succeeded in making a sufficiently good impression of ourselves so that others say, 'This person has practised Bodhichitta very well,' then this may be regarded as one kind of testimony. But if we think about it, we can see that unless such people have the ability to read our minds, our mental processes are hidden from them; they cannot know whether or not we have applied all the antidotes. Therefore we should examine ourselves, to see whether in fact we are less angry, less attached to ego, and whether we have been able to practise the exchange of happiness and suffering. That is the main testimony that we should rely on. We should live in such a way that we always have a clear conscience.

Milarepa said: 'My religion is to have nothing to be ashamed of when I die.' But the majority of people do not give any importance to this way of thinking. We pretend to be very calm and subdued and are full of sweet words, so that ordinary people, not knowing our thoughts, say, 'This is a real Bodhisattva.' But it is only our outward behaviour that they see.

The important thing is not to do anything that we might have to regret later on. Therefore we should examine ourselves honestly. Unfortunately, our ego-clinging is so gross that, even if we do possess some small quality, we think that we are wonderful. On the other hand, if we have some great defect, we do not even notice it. There is a saying that, 'On the peak of pride the water of good qualities does not stay.' So, we should be very meticulous. If, after thoroughly examining ourselves, we can put our hands on our hearts and honestly think, 'My actions are all right,' then that is a sign that we are getting some experience in Mind Training. We should then be glad that our practice has gone well, and determine to do even better in the future, just as did the Bodhisattvas of former times. By every means we should try to generate the antidote more and more and to act in such a way that we are at peace with ourselves.

Always be sustained by cheerfulness.

On account of the strength of their Mind Training, the Kadampa Masters were always able to look on the bright side of things no matter what happened to them. Even if they contracted leprosy they would continue to be cheerful, happy in the knowledge that leprosy brings a painless death. Of course, leprosy is one of the worst of all diseases, but we should be resolved that, even if we were to catch it, we would continue to practise the exchange of happiness for sorrow, taking upon ourselves the sufferings of all who have fallen victim to that affliction.

Strengthened by this attitude, we should decide that, by virtue of the Mind Training, we will be able to take onto the path whatever difficult situations arise. If we are able to do this with confidence, it is a sign that we are experienced in the practice; and we will be happy come what may. In addition, we must take upon ourselves, and experience, the sufferings of others. When others are having to endure physical and mental illness, or are confronted with all sorts of adversity, we should want to take it all upon ourselves. And we should do so without any hope or fear. 'But if the sufferings of others really do come upon me, what shall I do?'—second thoughts like this should be completely banished from our minds.

> *With experience you can practise even when distracted.*

Experienced riders do not fall off their horses. In the same way, when unexpected harm or sudden difficulties befall us, if love and compassion, rather than annoyance, come welling up in us of their own accord—in other words, if uncomfortable situations can be used to advantage in our lives, that is a sign that we have accomplished something in the Mind Training. So it is vitally important for us to continue in our efforts.

Experiences like this indicate a familiarity with the Mind Training; they do not, however, mean that the work is finished. For even if such signs occur, we should continue in our endeavour, becoming more thoroughly adept and always joyful. A mind, moreover, which has been subdued and calmed through practice will naturally reveal itself in external activities. As with the different proverbs, 'When you see the ducks, you know the water's near' and 'No smoke without fire.' So too, Bodhisattvas can be recognised by outward signs.

> Calmness and serenity
> Will show your wisdom;
> Freedom from defiled emotions
> Will display your progress on the path;
> Your perfection will be manifest
> Through virtue done in dreams.
> A Bodhisattva is revealed by what he does.

Signs like this will arise in us as well, but they do not mean that there is nothing more for us to do.

VI

THE COMMITMENTS OF THE MIND TRAINING

Always train in three common points.

THESE general points are: to be consistent in the pledges of the Mind Training, not to be affected and theatrical and not to have double standards.

Consistency in the Mind Training. We should give happiness without regret and attribute all good things and qualities to others. We should take upon ourselves all their sorrow and unwanted situations, accepting suffering with joy. We should strive to free others from their pain, offering them happiness, great or small, sincerely and without second thoughts, in particular towards those who do us harm. And we should not neglect the lesser commitments with the excuse that 'we are practising the Mind Training.' Never forgetting the Mind Training, we should nevertheless respect and practise all the commitments, from the Shravakayana to the Vajrayana, that we have promised, drawing them all together into a single way of life. If we are able to do this, it is an extraordinary stepping stone to all the paths of the great vehicle. Therefore let us observe all the vows with equal attention.

Not being affected. In our daily lives, our words should correspond with the actual way we practise Dharma. Moreover, we should avoid doing things in front of others in order to give the impression that we are renunciates and which therefore redound to our advantage. And we should refrain from actions calculated to make others think that we are free from ego-clinging, such as a cavalier attitude with regard to traditional religious sensibilities, or ostentatiously touching lepers or others suffering from contagious diseases. We should not do anything that the Kadampa masters would not do.

No double standards. For example, we might be patient with the harm that human beings inflict on us but intolerant when it comes to the attacks of spirits and demons. We should be courteous to the poor as well as to the powerful. We should avoid attachment to relatives and animosity toward enemies, ridding ourselves of all partiality. But let us be especially respectful towards poor, humble people of no importance. Do not be partial! Love and compassion should be universal toward all beings.

Change your attitude and maintain it firmly.

From time without beginning, our ego clinging has caused us to wander in samsara; it is the root of all our sufferings, it is indeed the culprit.

Considering others to be more important than ourselves, we should give up our self-cherishing attitudes and decide to act without hypocrisy, emulating in body, speech and mind, the behaviour of friends who live their lives according to the teachings. Mind Training should be engaged in discreetly. It should not be done with external show, in a way that attracts attention and creates a reputation; it should act as the inward antidote to our self-clinging and defiled emotions. We should bring our minds to ripeness without anybody knowing.

Do not discuss infirmities.

We should not discuss the handicaps of others. If they cannot see or walk well, if they are not intelligent or even if they have transgressed their vows, we should not call them blind, cripples, idiots, etc. In brief, we should not say anything that is unpleasant for others to hear.

Do not have opinions on other people's actions.

When we see defects in others, people in general but particularly those who have entered the Dharma, who are disciples of the same Teacher, or who, being clothed in the banner of the monastic robes, are the support for the offerings of gods and men alike, we should understand that it is the impurity of our perception which is at fault. When we look into a mirror, we see a dirty face because our own face is dirty. In the same way, the defects of others are nothing but our impure way of seeing them. By thinking in this way, we should try to rid ourselves of this perception of the faults of others, and cultivate the attitude whereby the whole of existence, all appearances, are experienced as pure.

Work on the strongest of your defilements first.

We should scrutinize ourselves and examine which of our defiled emotions is the most powerful. If desire is strongest, we should try to concentrate upon its antidote, which is ugliness. If anger is to the fore, we should try to generate the remedy of patience. If by nature we are inclined to ignorance and dullness, we should exert ourselves in the cultivation of wisdom. If we are jealous, we should work to develop equanimity. In this endeavour to subdue these defilements, we should concentrate all our

Dharma practice. For if we are able to free ourselves of the grosser defilements, the lesser ones will also naturally subside.

Give up hoping for results.

The general effect of Mind Training is to free the practitioner from hope and fear. We should practise the exchange of happiness and suffering without expecting any reward. We should not hope, for example, that because of our practice many non-human beings will gather round, obeying us and displaying miracles, and that people, prompted by them, will also serve us, bringing us wealth and influence. We should rid ourselves of all selfish ideas and ulterior motives, such as working for others but with the wish for our own individual liberation or rebirth in a pure realm.

Give up poisoned food.

There is a saying: 'Wholesome deeds performed with selfish aims are just like poisoned food.' Poisoned food might look delicious and even taste good, but it quickly leads to certain death.

Thinking of an enemy as someone to be hated, thinking of a friend as someone to be loved, being jealous of others' happiness and good fortune: all this is rooted in ego clinging. And wholesome actions, infiltrated by a clinging to the 'I' conceived as something real and solid, turn to poison. We should try to forsake all selfcentredness.

Do not be hidebound by a sense of duty.

Faithful to the memory of their parents, people exchange favours—or pursue vendettas against their ancestral enemies. We should not allow ourselves to be ruled by this kind of prejudice.

Do not meet abuse with abuse.

If people say to us, 'You are not a good practitioner. Your vows are useless,' we should not respond, by pointing out their defects, for instance telling a blind man that he is blind, or a lame man that he is a cripple. If we act like this, then both parties will be angry. Therefore let us not utter a word that will harm or make others unhappy. When things are not going well, we should not blame anyone else.

Do not wait in ambush.

'Ambush,' in this case, means remembering the harm done to us by others and biding our time for a moment of weakness when we might strike back, seeking the help of the powerful or even resorting to witchcraft, and so on. We should relinquish any thoughts of this kind.

Do not strike at weaknesses.

Do not strike at the weak points of others or do anything which will cause them suffering. In the same way, do not recite destructive mantras which will harm non-human beings.

Do not lay the dzo's[25] burden on an ox's back.

The meaning of this is that we should never allow any injury or blame that we deserve to fall on others. An ox cannot carry the load of dzo. Moreover, we should endeavour to keep from harming the poor and the weak, by burdening them with heavier taxes than others, and so on. All such evil actions should be completely forsaken.

Do not praise with hidden motives.

If, for example we hold some wealth in common with other people, we should not cajole them with flattery into giving us their share, saying things like, 'You are famous for your kindness,' or 'By being generous, you will accumulate much merit.' We should not do anything in fact to make someone happy so that he might give us money: all that kind of thing must be abandoned.

Do not misuse the remedy.

We would be misusing the remedy if we were to take upon ourselves the misfortunes of others, but with a wish for personal happiness or that others might say of us that we are patient and loving Bodhisattvas, trying thus to build up for ourselves a good reputation. We should free ourselves of all such intentions and never assume the misfortunes of others for these reasons.

Another example of this kind of behaviour would be wanting to practise the Mind Training in order to be cured from a disease, or out of fear of ghosts and spirits. This is just like practising exorcism with the intention of punishing the spirits with wrathful mantras; it is something which should be completely abandoned. We should not reduce the mind training to the level of mere sorcery by trying to use it as a means of repelling evil influences. Evil spirits and ghosts harm others because they are deluded. We should not practise the Mind Training against them, but to free them from their bad karma. When they create obstacles, we should practise *chöd* with compassion; then they will not harm us. Our practice should be the antidote only for our own negative emotions.

Do not bring a god down to the level of a demon.

Worldly people use their religion, in order to have success in business, to acquire power and situations of prosperity; but if they fall sick, lose their position and so on, they think their gods are displeased and begin to think of them as demons.

If through the Mind Training we become proud and boastful, it will be as Gampopa[26] once said: Dharma not practised properly, will bring us down to the lower realms. If we become pretentious and conceited, we will certainly not be practising Dharma. Because of our pride, the Mind Training, instead of taming us as it should, will make us all the more hard and obstinate. We will become so arrogant that, even if we were to see a Buddha flying in the sky, or someone suffering greatly, with his intestines hanging out, we would feel neither devotion for the qualities of the Buddhas nor compassion for the sufferings of beings. The whole point of the Dharma will have been missed. It does not help to station soldiers at the western gate, when the enemy is in the east. When we have a liver complaint, we should take the proper liver medicine. When we have fever, again, we should take the appropriate remedy. If the medicine we take is unsuited to the illness we have, our condition will be all the worse. In the same way, we should apply the teachings so that they act as an antidote to our ego-clinging. Towards everyone we should consider ourselves as the humblest of servants, taking the lowest place. We should try really very hard to be modest and self-forgetting.

Do not take advantage of suffering.

If, at the death of relatives or friends, we were to try everything in order to get possession of their belongings, food, money, books etc.; if our sponsor were to fall ill or die, and we were to go to his house with the intention of performing ceremonies in the hope of being remunerated; or if again, at the death of a meditator on our own level, we were to feel pleased at being henceforth without a rival—or at the death of an enemy, to feel that we were no longer threatened, we would indeed be taking advantage of the suffering of others. That is something we must not do.

VII

GUIDELINES FOR THE MIND TRAINING

HERE is some further advice on how to apply the Mind Training to ourselves, consolidating and enhancing our compassion and Bodhichitta.

Do everything with one intention.

We should try to think altruistically. For example, as regards our food and the way we dress ourselves, when we are given something delicious to eat, we should think: 'May all beings also have good food to enjoy; would that I were able to share this meal with all who are hungry.' Likewise, when we receive good clothes, let us think, 'May everyone have good clothes like these.'

Apply one remedy in all adversity.

In the course of our Mind Training, when we fall sick or are a prey to negative forces; when we are unpopular and suffer from a bad reputation, when we have increasingly strong emotions and lose the desire for Mind Training: at such times we should reflect that in this world there are many who are afflicted in the same way and whose conduct is at variance with the teaching. Even if we were to explain the doctrine and the methods to develop good qualities, nobody would want to listen—our words would fall upon deaf ears. On the other hand, people take to lying and stealing naturally without having to be taught. Their actions conflict with their desires—where else could they be but in samsara and the lower realms? We should therefore feel sorry for them and, taking all their defects upon ourselves, we should pray that their negative actions might cease and that they might start upon the path of Freedom. We should pray that they might become weary of samsara and want to turn from it, that they might generate Bodhichitta and that all the effects of their laziness and indifference to the Dharma might fall upon us. In other words, we should practise the exchange of good for evil.

> *Two things to be done, at the start and at the*
> *finish.*

In the morning, on awaking, we should make the following pledge: 'Throughout the whole of today, I will remember Bodhichitta. Eating, dressing, meditating, wherever I go, I will practise it constantly. Should it slip my mind, I will remind myself. Mindful of it, I will not allow myself to wander into states of anger, desire or ignorance.' We should make a concerted effort to keep this vow and at night before going to sleep, we should examine ourselves as to how much we have been able to generate Bodhichitta, how much we have been able to help others and whether all our actions have been in accordance with the teachings.

If we find that we have acted against the teachings, we should reflect that though we have entered the Buddhadharma and received the teachings of the Great Vehicle from our Teacher, we are still incapable of putting them into practice. This is because for countless lives we have turned our backs on the doctrine. If we carry on like this, there will be no end to our wandering in samsara and the lower realms. We should chide ourselves in this way, confessing the day's faults and resolving that, from the next day onwards, within twenty four hours, or a month, or at least within the year, we will have some signs of improvement. We should steel ourselves so as not to be daunted by the work of abandoning defects. If during the day our actions have not been contrary to the teachings and we have maintained an altruistic attitude, then we should be happy, thinking, 'Today has been a useful day, I have remembered what my Teacher has taught me and this is to accomplish his wishes. Tomorrow I will do better than today, and even better the day after.' This is how to ensure the growth of our Bodhichitta.

Bear whichever of the two occurs.

Through faith in the Three Jewels and the practice of generosity, it could happen that, by way of karmic fruit, we become rich, gain a high position in society and so on. This might lead us to think, 'I am rich, I am important, I am the best, I have come out on top.' If we practitioners have this kind of arrogance, our clinging to this life will increase and a demon will enter our hearts. If, on the other hand, we manage to enjoy happiness, possessions and influence without pride, we will understand that they are nothing but illusions, insubstantial dreams, all of which will one day fade away. For as it is said of all compounded things, 'what is accumulated will be used up; what is raised up will fall; what is born will die; what is joined together will separate.'

'Who knows,' we should tell ourselves, 'perhaps tomorrow I shall have to say goodbye to all of this. Therefore, I will offer to my Teachers and the Three Jewels the best of my contentment and possessions. May they accept it with joy and bless me so that I might have no obstacles on the path. All of it is just a pleasant dream, but may all

beings experience such happiness as mine, and even
more.'

On the other hand, when we are in such poor shape
that we cannot even practise, that we have strong emotions and feelings of irritation, fighting and quarrelling
with everyone, we should reflect: 'I know that everything
is illusory; I will therefore not allow myself to be carried
away by my feelings. I will not be a coward! I will shoulder the weakness, poverty, illness and death of other
beings.' To put it briefly, we should be able to think that,
provided that the precious Bodhichitta does not decrease
in us, who cares if we have to go to the lower realms, who
cares if we lose our possessions? Come what may, like
beggars with a precious jewel, we will not forsake
Bodhichitta.

Even if it costs you your life, defend the two.

This refers in general to the vows of the Shravakayana,
Mahayana and Vajrayana and particularly to the special
vows of Mind Training. The vows of the Mind Training
are: to give victory and benefit to others and to take all
loss and failure, especially that of our enemies, upon
ourselves. If we act accordingly, the Mind Training will
take effect. On the other hand, if we fail to practise these
two vows, we will achieve neither the short term benefit
of happiness in this life and rebirth in the realms of
human beings or of gods, nor the long term benefit of
rebirth in a pure field. We should therefore observe these
vows at all costs, just as we guard our eyes from thorns
when we are walking through the woods.

Train yourself in three hard disciplines.

These are the difficult practices of mindfulness, of
expulsion and of 'interrupting the flow.'

As for the first of these, the difficult practice of mind-fulness, it is necessary to recognize afflictive emotions as soon as they arise and it is hard, at first, to remain sufficiently aware to be able to do this. However, when negative emotions arise, we should identify them as anger, desire or stupidity. Even when emotions have been recognized, it is not easy to drive them out with the antidote. If, for instance, an uncontrollably strong emotion comes over us, so that we feel helplessly in its power, we should nevertheless confront it and question it. Where are its weapons? Where are its muscles? Where is its great army and its political strength? We will see that emotions are just insubstantial thoughts, by nature empty: they come from nowhere, they go nowhere, they remain nowhere. When we are able to repel our defiled emotions, there comes the difficult practice of 'interrupting the flow.' This means that, on the basis of the antidote described, defiled emotions are eliminated just like a bird flying through the air: no trace is left behind. These are practices in which we should really strive.

Have recourse to three essential factors.

The three essential factors on which the accomplishment of the Dharma depends are: to meet with a qualified teacher; by receiving his instructions, to cultivate the correct attitude; and, finally, to have the necessary material conditions.

If we do not follow a genuine master, we will never know how to practise the teachings. If the Buddha had not turned the Wheel of Dharma, we would not know what actions we should do and what actions we should refrain from. How can we, who have not had the fortune to meet the Buddha in person, practise the path of liberation if we do not follow a master? How else could we recognize paths which are mistaken and inferior? Moreover, just as we treat stiff leather with oil to make it smooth and supple, so too we should practise the teachings correctly, with a calm and docile attitude, undisturbed by afflictive emotions. Finally, living in the realm of desire, as we do, we find it impossible to practise the Dharma if we lack food to fill our stomachs and clothes to cover us against the wind.

If we have these three essential factors complete we should be happy at the thought we have all that is necessary to practise the teachings. It is as though we have been equipped with a good horse for an uphill journey—the way will be without difficulty. And we should pray that all beings might be just as fortunate.

If, however, we do not possess all of these essential factors, we should reflect that though we have entered the Buddhadharma and received plenty of teachings and instructions, we still lack the conditions suitable for practice.

As a matter of fact, there are many disciples who are unable to practise properly because of this shortcoming. They have what is known as 'good karma going wrong.' As was explained before, 'Old yogis getting rich; old teachers getting married.' We should feel sorry for such people and pray from our hearts that the cause of their not having such favourable conditions might ripen upon us and that, as a result, their situation might be improved.

> *Meditate on three things that must not*
> *deteriorate.*

These are devotion, enthusiasm and Bodhichitta.

Devotion to our Teacher is the source of all the qualities of the Mahayana. If the Buddha himself were to appear in front of us and we were lacking in the devotion to see his qualities, his blessings would be unable to enter us. The Buddha's kinsmen, Devadatta and Lekpe Karma, failed to see him as an enlightened being; they mistook and criticized all his actions and, abandoning themselves to their jealousy, were reborn in the realms of hell. If we have perfect confidence and devotion to see as positive all the activities of our Teacher—even if he is not a superior being—the wisdom of realization will effortlessly arise in us, as it did in Sadaprarudita,[27] who through devotion to his Teacher realized the nature of emptiness. Thus our devotion is something that we must never allow to deteriorate.

This Mind Training is the quintessence of the Mahayana. It is the butter which comes from the milk of the doctrine. Of all the eighty four thousand teachings expounded by Buddha, if we can but practise the Bodhichitta, that is sufficient. Actually, it is like an indispensable medicine: it is something we simply cannot do without. It is the distilled essence of all the teachings. To hear it is fortunate indeed, and great is the kindness of the teacher who explains it, for its greatness is simply inconceivable. By contrast, if we were to use the instructions on the four tantric activities,[28] for the purpose of lengthening our lives or getting the better of our enemies, bandits and so on, we should be working only for our present lives.

But this precious teaching of Bodhichitta! If only we can experience it just a little in our minds! One instant of negative thought will bring us suffering for innumerable ages. Conversely, one instant of Bodhichitta can obliterate the effects of all the evil acts of infinite kalpas. All accumulations of merit and all acts of purification are gathered in a single thought of Bodhichitta. Any action grounded in this attitude partakes of the ocean-like activity of the Mahayana. Therefore we should practise Bodhichitta with a joy and enthusiasm which we must never allow to lessen.

To accustom oneself to Bodhichitta is like keeping a garden neat, without undergrowth, insects, lumps of wood and weeds. Let us practise it, bringing together all the qualities of the greater and lesser vehicles, so that we are like containers gradually filled with grain, or pots with drops of water. Whether we practise Pratimoksha, the Bodhisattva training, or the stages of generation and completion of the Mantrayana, all that we do should act as a support for our vows of Bodhichitta. Even if we practise the Mantrayana, it should uphold and confirm our commitment as Bodhisattvas.

Whatever we do, listening to the teachings, contemplating or meditating upon them, we should take it all as an aid in our training. If we are able to use the Bodhichitta to bring everything onto the path, wholesome states of mind and positive thoughts will develop extraordinarily. By using the antidote, we should reverse all negative emotions that have so far arisen. In that way we should keep the Bodhichitta as our constant friend.

Three things maintain inseparably.

Our body, speech and mind should always be engaged in positive activity. When we are performing virtuous actions such as prostrations, circumambulations and the like, our speech and mind should be in harmony with our bodily movements. When accumulating positive actions of speech, recitation for instance, our body and our mind should also be engaged. If we undertake some positive mental act, the body and the speech should also be in attendance. For example, if, while performing prostrations or circumambulations, we chatter, or entertain a lot of negative emotions, this is just like eating polluted food. Therefore, while performing virtuous actions, our body, speech and mind should act inseparably and in unison.

Train impartially in every field;
Your training must be deep and all-pervading.

We should practise the Mind Training impartially without picking or choosing, and in relation to everything, whether animate or inanimate. We should practise so that whatever thoughts arise, they will serve as a path for the Mind Training, rather than being occasions for hindrances. Let this not be something that we merely talk about, but something deep within our hearts which we actually do.

Always meditate on what is unavoidable.

We should constantly meditate on difficulties that we cannot escape. Towards people, for instance, who do us harm, who want to compete with us, who are at one moment friendly but who suddenly turn against us unprovoked, or towards people who for no apparent reason (due to our karma) we simply do not like, we should try to generate the Bodhichitta even more intensely, especially when it is difficult.

We should serve and reverence our elders, parents and teachers. As Guru Padmasambhava said, 'Do not be a sorrow to your elders; serve them with respect.' If we help them and those who are in need of help, we are treading the path of the Bodhisattvas. We should give up whatever is at variance with that attitude.

Do not be dependent on external factors.

When we have enough food and clothes, enjoy good health, have whatever we need and are without troubles of any sort, we should not become attached to these benefits nor dependent on them. Conversely, when we do not enjoy such good conditions, and when everything is going badly, we should use such a situation as a trigger for our courage and take them as the Bodhisattva path. We should not give up when conditions are difficult; on the contrary, that is precisely when we should practise the twofold Bodhichitta, bringing all our experiences onto the path.

This time, do what is important.

Throughout our many lifetimes in the past, we may have taken many different forms. We have been rich. We have been beaten by our enemies, and lost everything. We have had all the pleasures of the gods. We have been victims of political oppression. We have been lepers or have suffered from other diseases. All those experiences of happiness and suffering have brought us nothing. But now, in this present life, we have entered the path set forth by the Buddha, we have met many learned and accomplished spiritual teachers: this time we must make such circumstances meaningful and do what is important.

If a merchant, visiting an isle of jewels, were to return empty handed without his cargo of gems, he would be ashamed to show his face in public. It is the same for us, who at this very moment, have such favourable conditions for the practice. If we can give rise to genuine Bodhichitta, it does not matter if we are poor, unknown and of no account.

The Dharma has two aspects: exposition and practice. Exposition is only the work of the mouth, and many there are who do not practise the teachings explained. As the saying goes: 'Many have heard the doctrine but those who implement it are few. Even those who have practised a little, are sidetracked and get lost.' As far as the Dharma is concerned, practice is more important than teaching and talking about it; the Dharma is something that we really have to *do*. Furthermore, we may recite millions of mantras, and do any number of good works, but if our minds are distracted, nothing beneficial will come of it; the teachings will not have benefited us and Bodhichitta will have had no chance to grow. Let us adopt Bodhichitta, therefore, above all other practices.

As it is said:

> One deity, Chenrezig, embodies all Buddhas;
> One mantra, the six syllables, embodies all mantras;
> One Dharma, Bodhichitta, embodies all practices of
>   the development and completion stages.
> Knowing the one which liberates all, recite the six
>   syllable mantra.

Bodhichitta is thus the chief of practices; it is better moreover to follow single-mindedly the instructions received from our Teachers than to practise on the basis of our own book-learning and intelligence. To the extent that they are processed and refined, gold and diamonds become pure and proportionately more precious. So too through the assiduous practice of the instructions received from our Teacher, our understanding of them will become increasingly profound. The Buddha himself said, 'Treat my words like gold, cutting, melting and refining; examine my doctrine well, for it is not to be accepted simply out of respect for me.' Just as with the smelting and refinement of gold, likewise the teaching of Buddha: by listening, we gain an understanding, which, the more we meditate, will become increasingly profound and vast. It is most important therefore to practise with a steady concentration. Of all our activities, the most important is to sit and practise. We should not move around too much, we should just remain on our seat. We will only stumble if we get up! We should sit properly, not too stiffly, and remember that the best practitioners wear out their meditation cushions, not the soles of their shoes.

Indeed, to apply the antidote to the emotions is even more important than to leave our homeland. For, if, on leaving home, we have even stronger attachment, desire and anger, our actions have not helped, but only harmed, our practice. The most important thing, therefore, is to use the antidote.

> *Do not make mistakes.*

There are six errors or misconceptions which we should guard against.

Mistaken patience or endurance. Religious people, who bravely put up with hardships and persevere in the practice even though they have nothing in the way of food and clothing, suffering from cold and so on, may well be a sorry sight. They may in fact lack material possessions, but they do not need us to feel sorry for them. After all, their discomforts will be short lived and are the means through which they will finally come to liberation. Quite different from that sort of courage is the mistaken bravery of ordinary heroes who, in order to destroy their opponents and protect their own side, undergo unbearable hardships in the fight against their enemies, or suffer the cruel discipline and fury of their leaders.

Misplaced interest. It is also a mistake to be intent on the accumulation of wealth, power and comfort for this life at the expense of Dharma practice.

> If you wish to practise properly,
> Sustain yourself with Dharma,
> Your Dharma with a humble life,
> Your humble life with the thought of death,
> Your thought of death with a lonely cave.

Our intention should be to help all sentient beings, who have been our mothers, and to bring them to the state of Buddhahood. We should never be self-satisfied and rest on our laurels, thinking that we have meditated well, that we have done retreat and are familiar with the rituals, or that we can chant and know all there is to know about the practice. This is an obstacle on the path.

Taking delight in worldly pleasures instead of in the Dharma. This is also a mistake. 'Learning comes from listening to the teachings; evil is reversed through listening to the teachings; futile ways are shunned by listening to the teachings.' Bear this in mind. We should try to understand whether the teachings are expressed in the relative or the absolute sense, and we should make an effort to grasp the ultimate meaning beyond the words. Then we should practise it with an undivided heart. That is how to make sure progress. However, having experienced a taste of the Dharma, most 'experts,' armed with their intellectual knowledge, allow themselves to be sidetracked into arguments and disputes with opponents, all for worldly satisfaction. Their taste of Dharma has played them false.

Misplaced compassion. It is a mistake to feel sorry for practitioners who endure a lot of difficulties for the sake of the Dharma, staying in lonely mountain hermitages without much food or warm clothing. It is incorrect to worry and think, 'These poor practitioners! They are going to die of starvation!' By contrast, the ones we should really feel sorry for are those who commit evil actions, such as army leaders and military heroes who kill hundreds and thousands of people, and whose hatred will drag them down into the realms of hell. We should show compassion to those who need it.

Being helpful in the wrong way. It is a mistake, too, to introduce our relations and dependants to worldly happiness and success instead of bringing them into contact with the Dharma. If we really care for them, we should help them to meet religious teachers and instruct them in the practice. Day by day, we should show them how to tread the path of liberation. Good people are like medicinal trees: whoever frequents them becomes good also. But if, by contrast, we teach people how to do business, how to trick others and stand up to their enemies, they will become as vicious as we are.

Rejoicing inappropriately. It is wrong to rejoice at the sufferings of enemies instead of at whatever is joyful and virtuous. By contrast, when people engage in work for any kind of good cause, or when Dharma-practitioners undertake innumerable *nyungne* fasts,[29] when they do a lot of work, building temples, constructing stupas and images or printing books, we should pray: 'In this life and their lives to come, may they always practise virtue, may their good actions bring about the birth of Bodhichitta in their minds.' This is the proper way to rejoice. But if, on the contrary, we feel pleasure and satisfaction when someone we dislike is punished by his superiors, or even killed—thinking that he only got what was coming to him, we are rejoicing wrongly.

These, then, are six wrong actions that we should forsake if we wish to follow the unmistaken way.

Be consistent in your practice.

When we are content and our lives are going well, we feel inclined to practise; but when, for instance, we are hungry and have nothing to eat, we lose interest. This is because we lack perfect confidence in the teachings. As the saying goes, 'Well fed and warm in the sun: that's when we look like practitioners. But when things go wrong, we are very ordinary people. The Dharma and our minds never seem to mingle. Bless us with the proper attitude!' And it is said too, 'Meditators whose behaviour has drifted into ordinary ways will never be free. Reciting many mantras for the sake of appearances will not help us on the path.'

Be zealous in your training.

Let us train ourselves wholeheartedly, completely saturating ourselves with the Mind Training: sometimes meditating on emptiness, sometimes on detachment from this life and sometimes on compassion towards beings. Through investigation and examination, we should endeavour to practise the methods of cultivating the Mind Training more and more.

Free yourself by analysis and testing.

Let us first examine which of our emotions is strongest. Then let us make a concerted effort to generate its antidote, investigating whether the emotion increases when we are confronted by certain specific situations. We should observe whether it arises or not, recognize it and, with the help of the antidote, rid ourselves of it, persevering until it no longer arises.

Don't take what you do too seriously.

If we help others by providing them with food and clothing, by freeing them from prison, or by promoting them to some position of importance, it should not be with the expectation of some kind of recognition. If we practise intensely and for a long time, or if we are knowledgeable and disciplined, we should not expect to be respected for it. If, on the other hand, we find that others know a great deal, we should pray for them to become really learned; if they are very disciplined, we should pray for them to be like the disciples at the time of

Buddha; if we see people practising, we should pray that their minds be blended with the practice, that their practice be without obstacle and that their paths might lead to the final goal. That is how we should meditate, caring more for others than for ourselves. But if we manage to do so, we should not congratulate ourselves on having done something great or extraordinary. 'Do not rely on other human beings; just pray to the yidam.' Such was the advice of Radreng.[30] Therefore, do not count on others for help with food, clothing, etc. Rather have a confident faith in the Three Jewels. As it is said: 'Trusting in the Teacher is the ultimate refuge, working for the benefit of others is the ultimate Bodhichitta, therefore do not brag about your accomplishments.' We should always have this attitude, because if we depend on others, the results may not be as we wish...

Do not be bad tempered.

If it happens that we are slighted in public, we should never think to ourselves that despite the fact that we are such good practitioners, people have no regard for us and do not come to pay respects or to receive our blessings. We should not react with annoyance and harsh words. At the moment, because we have not used the teachings as an antidote for ego-clinging, our patience and forbearance are more fragile than a blister and we are as irritable as a bear with a sore head. All that because we have failed to use the instructions as an antidote.

Do not be temperamental.

Because of its transparency, a crystal ball takes on the colour of whatever it is standing on. In the same way, there are some practitioners, who, if they are given a lot of money, will have all sorts of positive thoughts. 'Oh, this is such a kind sponsor,' they will say. But if they get nothing, they will say bad things and hold a grudge. We should not be swayed by such trivial things.

Do not expect to be rewarded.

If we have been of help to others or have managed to practise, we should not expect thanks, praise or fame. If we practise the two Bodhichittas all our lives, perform our meditation and post-meditation properly, and if we mingle our minds with the view of meditation, our experience in day to day life will not be ordinary. Furthermore, if we are not distracted in our daily lives, this will help our meditation to progress. If, however, we meditate single-mindedly during the sessions, but afterwards are completely distracted, we will not gain confidence in the view of meditation. Conversely, if we develop virtuous habits in post-meditation but during the meditation session engage in useless activities, again our practice will be meaningless. Therefore we should make sure to train ourselves correctly.

CONCLUSION

This distilled essence of instruction,
Which transmutes the upsurge of the five
degenerations
Into the path of enlightenment,
Was handed down by Serlingpa.

THE five degenerations are as follows: in degenerate times, 1) beings die early, tormented by famine, disease, weapons and war; 2) they have evil dispositions, they are without inclination to virtue and are thoroughly opposed to the supreme Doctrine; 3) the lives of such beings are brief; 4) depraved emotions are powerful; 5) ideas and views are coarse and mistaken.

In these times the causes of happiness are very few. Beings accumulate evil actions, the various effects of which bring suffering. Adverse conditions such as those just listed are powerfully present. It is like having to cross a forest in which the branches are closely matted together! Yet, through meditating on the Mind Training, the harm one comes across, be it disease, the work of evil spirits, obstacles or slanders, all this can be used as the path to enlightenment, constantly increasing our virtue. It is just as when someone who knows what he is about, can

consume poisonous drugs so that they act as a life-sus-
taining medicine. He does not die from them, but is like
the peacock which grows in beauty and splendour, nour-
ished by its deadly food.

Every benefit derives from this precious Bodhichitta.
By means of it, we bring together all positive actions of
body, speech and mind, we mingle our minds with the
teachings and gain for ourselves and others all the happiness of both samsara and nirvana. By practising this
Mind Training well, it will not be long before we are able
to accomplish the abundant welfare of other beings and
ourselves.

> *Having roused the karma of past training,*
> *And feeling powerfully inspired,*
> *I disregarded suffering and censure*
> *And sought out the instructions to subdue my*
>   *ego-clinging;*
> *Though I may die, I shall now have no regret.*

The Master Chekawa Yeshe Dorje, a great king among
yogis, frequented many teachers of the Kadampa tradition.
Receiving this instruction, he further listened, reflected
and meditated, truly practising the Mind Training. He
reached that stage where, utterly devoid of self-cherishing, he truly cared for others more than himself.

> *At the kind request of Drakpa, the king of*
>   *Dharma*
> *And his devoted students,*
> *This jewel-like treasury of pith instructions*
> *Was revealed. May all beings practise*
> *And accomplish the twofold Bodhichitta.*

Repeatedly requested by the accomplished Mahayana
practitioner Drakpa Gyaltsen, these few words of explanation of the Seven Point Mind Training were written by

the monk Thogme in the lonely place of Ngulchu Dzong. Drakpa Gyaltsen used to tell his disciples, 'Do not think that Chenrezig is a person with four arms living on the Potala mountain; go to see the Lama who resides at Ngulchu Dzong and receive his teachings. There is nothing more to see in Chenrezig than there is in him.'

Bodhichitta was very strong in Ngulchu Thogme from his earliest youth. Once when he was a little child, he went outside to relieve himself. On his way back he caught sight of a bush covered in snow. Thinking it was a man, the little boy wrapped his clothes around the bush and came back into the house naked.

His mother asked him, 'Where are all your clothes?'

'There is a man outside who is freezing,' he replied. 'I put them over him.' His mother went outside and saw that it was only a bush.

That is the kind of Bodhisattva Ngulchu Thogme was. He truly practised and was fully experienced in the Bodhisattva way of life.

This training in Bodhichitta is the essence of the eighty four thousand teachings of Buddha. Even if we are at the moment unable to accomplish it perfectly, our practice of it will nevertheless contribute to the happiness of this life; in the future we will escape the lower realms and will be of great help to all those with whom we come into contact. There exist many teachings, profound and vast, such as Mahamudra and Dzogchen. But our mental capacity is small, we are without perseverance and lack sufficient respect and devotion to be freed through teachings such as these. Nonetheless, if we practise this Mind Training, we will experience great benefits. It is an extraordinary instruction, the very essence of the Bodhisattva teachings, and has been praised again and again. Therefore let us practise it without distraction.

May all the wishes for the good of beings, conceived by all the enlightened Buddhas from the beginning down to our very Teachers, be accomplished through the effort of making this text available! May it be auspicious!

NECTAR OF THE MIND

A Prayer of the Seven Point Mind Training

by

Jamyang Khyentse Wangpo

NECTAR OF THE MIND

A Prayer of the Seven Point Mind Training

The Seven Point Mind Training, pith-instructions of the supreme Kadampas who possessed the seven Divine Doctrines, is explained according to the tradition of Chekawa Yeshe Dorje in three Meritorious Acts.

THE FIRST ACT, MERITORIOUS AT THE BEGINNING

I
Title of the Prayer

Nectar of the Mind, a Prayer of the Seven Point Mind Training

II
The Praise

I bow to the Spiritual Friends of the Supreme Vehicle,
Source of everything good in samsara and nirvana.
By the gracious Lama's blessings
May my mind be purified with the three kinds of faith.

THE SECOND ACT, MERITORIOUS IN THE MIDDLE:
THE MAIN SUBJECT OF THE TEXT

I
The Preliminaries,
Foundation of the Teachings

By the gracious Lama's blessings,
Knowing how hard to obtain and how easily destroyed is this
*   precious human life,*
In all my actions, according to their karmic effect, may I try
*   to do what is right and avoid what is wrong*
And develop a genuine determination to be free from
*   samsara, as I train in the preliminaries.*

II
The Main Practice,
Training in Bodhichitta

By the gracious Lama's blessings,
May I purify the untruth of duality into the space of voidness
And practise the profound exchange of my own and others'
*   happiness and suffering ;*
Meditating continually on the two aspects of Bodhichitta.

III
Turning Adverse
Circumstances into the Path of Bodhichitta

By the gracious Lama's blessings,
May I see whatever adverse events and sufferings befall me
As tricks of the evil spirit of ego-clinging
And use them as the path of Bodhichitta.

IV
Applying this Practice throughout one's Life

By the gracious Lama's blessings,
May I condense my lifetime's practice into a single essence
By applying throughout my life the five powers of pure
*   determination, pure practice,*
Accumulation of merit, purification of obscurations, and
*   prayers of aspiration.*

V
The Signs of the Mind Training

By the gracious Lama's blessings,
When everything arises as the antidote to ego-clinging
And my mind finds freedom, with happiness and confidence
May I take all adverse circumstances as the path.

VI
The Commitments of the Mind Training

By the gracious Lama's blessings,
May I keep my promises, be free of hypocrisy,
Have no partiality and little outward show ;
Protecting the commitments of the mind training as I would
*   my own life.*

VII
The Precepts of the Mind Training

In essence, by the gracious Lama's blessings,
May I genuinely train my mind
According to all the precepts which further the two aspects
*   of Bodhichitta*
And attain realisation of the Supreme Vehicle within this
*   very lifetime.*

THE THIRD ACT, MERITORIOUS AT THE END

I
Dedication

By the merit of this heartfelt aspiration
To practice the Seven Point Mind Training,
Essence of the minds of the peerless Lord[31] and his disciples,
May all beings accomplish enlightenment

II
The Colophon

This prayer was made with one-pointed mind in front of glorious Atisha's precious image at Kyishö Nyethang by Jamyang Khyentse Wangpo, a carefree wanderer with supreme respect for the tradition of the precious Kadampas. May I be blessed to accomplish this prayer.

May virtue ensue !

NOTES

1   **Chenrezig**: Skt. Avalokiteshvara or Lokeshvara, the Bodhisattva of compassion, one of the 'Eight Close Sons' of the Buddha. He is considered as the essence of the Speech of all the Buddhas and the manifestation of their Compassion. He is one of the three Bodhisattvas (the other two being Mañjushri and Vajrapani) known as the Protectors of the Three Families. Finally he is the patron and protector of the Tibetan land and people.

2   **Ngulchu Thogme Zangpo**: (1295-1369) Disciple of the great Butön Rinpoche and a celebrated master of the Kadampa Tradition. He is the author of the 'Thirty Seven Practices of the Bodhisattvas.'

3   **Guru Rinpoche**: Otherwise known as Padmasambhava, or Orgyen Pema Jungne, the Lotus-born Master of Oddiyana. The great tantric master of unexampled wisdom and yogic power, invited to Tibet by the king Trisong Detsen to propagate the Dharma. Subjugating and converting the negative forces hostile to the Buddhist doctrine, he filled the country with his teachings, concealing many more in the form of Dharma Treasures for the benefit of later generations. He is venerated as the Second Buddha, and was prophesied by Shakyamuni himself.

4   **Nagarjuna**: (*klu sgrub*) (3rd century) Great Indian master and systematizer of the Prajñaparamita teachings, the founder of the Madhyamika school.

5   **Atisha Dipamkara**: (982-1054) Great Indian master and scholar, known in Tibet simply as *Jowo Je*, the Lord. He was one of the most renowned teachers of the university of Vikramashila and celebrated as a rigorous upholder of the monastic discipline. He spent the last twelve years of his life in Tibet where he taught widely, revivifying the Dharma after a period of savage persecution and contributing much to the work of translation of Buddhist texts into Tibetan.

6   **Chekawa Yeshe Dorje**: (1101-1175) Famous Kadampa geshe (or master). By systematizing the teachings of the Mind Training into seven points, he rendered them much more accessible and easier to propagate than had been the case before him.

7   **Vikramashila and Nalanda**: The two most famous Buddhist universities in India until the decline of the doctrine in its homeland at the end of the 12th century.

8   **Lhasa, Samye and Trandruk**: Three of the most important holy places in Tibet. Lhasa: capital of the country, seat of His Holiness the Dalai Lama, and site of famous temples such as the Jokhang, which contains the Jowo Rinpoche (see note 18); Samye: first monastery in Tibet founded in the 8th century by the king Trisong Detsen, Guru Rinpoche and the Abbot Shantarakshita; Trandruk: monastery in the south of Tibet founded by Songtsen Gampo, the first Buddhist king of Tibet.

9   **Milarepa**: (1052-1135) One of the most famous and beloved poets and yogis in Tibetan history. He was the disciple of Marpa the Translator who, in order to enable him to purify the negativity of killing certain members of his family by black magic, subjected him to years of trial before consenting to teach him. After receiving instruction, however, Milarepa spent the rest of his life meditating in mountain solitudes.

He attained supreme enlightenment and left behind him a rich heritage of poetry and songs of realization.

10 **Shantideva:** (690-740) Famous Indian master, of royal birth and member of the monastic university of Nalanda. Author of numerous works, of which the celebrated *Bodhicharyavatara*.

11 **Evil spirits:** From its earliest beginnings, Buddhism has always acknowledged the existence of non-human 'spirits', that is, beings not normally perceptible to the physical senses; and in the Tibetan tradition especially, reference is often made to evil spirits, ghosts etc. which are identified and categorized according to a complex demonology. They are explained however in different ways and with varying degrees of subtlety according to context. In so far as demons etc. are conceived of as sentient beings, caught in samsara and afflicted by suffering, they are, as this text frequently points out, suitable objects of our compassion. Quite often, however, and as frequently happens according to the traditional viewpoint, they are understood as personifications of psychic energies, perhaps more akin to the neuroses and complexes of modern western psychology - features, in other words, of our own minds and manifestations of our own karma. Khenpo Ngawang Pelzang has remarked: 'What we call a demon is not something with a gaping mouth or staring eyes. It is that which creates all the troubles of samsara and prevents us from attaining the state beyond suffering that is liberation; it is in short whatever injures our body or mind.'

12 **Patrul Rinpoche:** (1808-1887) Orgyen Jigme Chökyi Wangpo, also known as Dzogchen Palge Tulku or Dza Patrul. An extraordinary master born in the province of Kham in eastern Tibet. After studying at the feet of all the most famous masters of his time, he became a wandering hermit, living in mountain caves or under forest trees and possessing neither house nor monastery. He meditated incessantly on love and compassion which he considered as the roots of spiritual practice. He was a living embodiment of the Bodhisattva way of life and was considered to be an incarnation of

Shantideva. He was profoundly learned and gifted with a prodigious memory, and unanimously respected by all the schools of Tibetan Buddhism. He became one of the most eminent representatives of the Rimé, or non sectarian, movement which began during the nineteenth century. He is the author of the well known *Kunzang Lama'i Zhel Lung* translated into English as 'The Words of my Perfect Master.'

13   **Bodhicharyavatara**: (*spyod 'jug*) The great poem of Shantideva covering all the aspects of the Bodhisattva's way of life and Mahayana philosophy.

14   **Brahmin**: Member of the priestly caste, the highest of the four great castes of India.

15   **Pure Land of Dewachen**: The Pure Field of the Buddha Amitabha (Boundless Light). A Pure Field is a dimension or world manifested through the enlightened aspirations of a Buddha or Bodhisattva in conjunction with the meritorious energy of sentient beings. Beings reborn in a Pure Field are able to progress swiftly to enlightenment and never fall into the lower realms of samsara. It is to be understood, however, that anywhere, perceived as the pure manifestation of spontaneous Wisdom, is in fact a Pure Field.

16   **Adzom Drukpa**: (1842-1924) Disciple of Jamyang Khyentse Wangpo and master of the second Jamyang Khyentse Chökyi Lodrö, a teacher also of Dilgo Khyentse Rinpoche. He was a Tertön, or discoverer of Dharma Treasures (see footnote 3 on Guru Rinpoche), and a very important master in the transmission of the Nyingmapa teachings.

17   **Geshe Karak Gomchung**: Eleventh century Kadampa master and disciple of Potowa.

18   **Jowo Rinpoche**: Image of Buddha Shakyamuni at the age of twelve, enshrined in the Jokhang, the central temple in Lhasa. This image, said to be blessed by Buddha himself, was brought to Tibet by one of the wives of king Songtsen Gampo.

19   **Buddha Shakyamuni**: The universal Buddha of our time, the fourth of the thousand Buddhas of the present kalpa.

20   **Abbot Shantarakshita**: Also known as Khenpo Bodhisattva, great master of the Mahayana and abbot of Nalanda. He was invited to Tibet by the king Trisong Detsen to help in the propagation of the Dharma and the building of the monastery of Samye.

21   **Vajrapani**: One of the eight close sons of the Buddha, the essence of the mind of all the Buddhas and the manifestation of their power (see footnote 1).

22   **Dromtönpa**: (1005-1064) Principle Tibetan disciple of Atisha, founder of the Kadampa school and builder of the monastery of Radreng.

23   **Langri Tangpa**: (1054-1123) Kadampa master, disciple of Potowa, author of the 'Eight Verses on the Mind Training.' Founder of the monastery of Langthang.

24   **Marpa**: (1012-1097) Great translator and Tibetan master, disciple of Drogmi, Naropa, Maitripa and other great siddhas. He brought back from India many scriptures and texts and founded the Kagyupa school of Tibetan Buddhism.

25   **Dzo**: A cross between a yak and a cow, an extremely powerful animal, much stronger than an ox.

26   **Gampopa**: (1079-1153) Also known as Dhagpo Rinpoche, the most famous disciple of Milarepa and founder of the Kagyu monastic lineage.

27   **Sadaprarudita**: Name of a great Bodhisattva in the time of the Buddha Dharmodgata, renowned for his courage and endurance in his quest for the doctrine.

28   **Four tantric activities**: (*phrin las rnam bzhi*) Sometimes referred to as the four types of enlightened activity. They are pacification, increase or enrichment, attraction and liberation (i.e. the forceful sending of the consciousness to a higher level of existence).

29   **Nyungne:** (*bsnyungs gnas*) Name of a strenuous purificatory practice associated with the Bodhisattva Chenrezig. It entails recitation of mantra, strict fasting and prostrations.

30   **Radreng:** Dromtönpa, see note 21.

31   **Lord Atisha:** See note 5.

GLOSSARY

Alaya: This Sanskrit term means 'storehouse.' It is rendered in Tibetan by the words *'kun gzhi,'* the literal sense of which is 'foundation of all things,' and indicates the basis equally of the mind and of phenomena, both pure and impure. The word has different meanings in different contexts and should be understood accordingly. Sometimes, it is synonymous with the Buddha-nature or Dharmakaya. Most often, however, it refers to a neutral state of dualistic but unconscious mind, which acts as the receptacle, so to speak, of the mental imprints of all the actions of body, speech or mind.

Arhat: (*dgra bcom pa*) Literally, 'One who has destroyed the enemies.' The enemies referred to are the *kleshas* or afflictive emotions which are vanquished through the practice of the teachings of the root vehicle or Shravaka-yana/Hinayana. Arhats achieve liberation from the sufferings of samsara, but because their realisation of emptiness is not perfect, they are unable to remove the subtle veils of attachment to phenomenal reality, which are the obstacles to omniscience. They have yet to enter the Mahayana in order to progress towards the supreme goal of Buddhahood.

Bardo: (*bar do*) Literally, 'between two,' i.e. the intermediate state. There are several kinds of bardo, but most often, the term is used to refer to the intermediate state occurring between death and rebirth.

Bodhichitta: (*byang chub sems*) The Mind of Enlightenment. This is a key word in the Mahayana. On the relative level, it is the wish to attain Buddhahood for the sake of all beings, as well as the practice necessary to do this. On the absolute level, it is the direct insight in the ultimate nature of self and phenomena.

Bodhisattva: (*byang chub sems dpa'*) A practitioner on the path to Buddhahood, training in the practice of compassion and the six transcendent perfections, who has vowed to attain enlightenment for the sake of all beings. The Tibetan translation of this term means literally a 'hero of the enlightened mind.'

Buddha: (*sangs rgyas*) One who has removed the two veils (the veil of afflictive emotions, which is the cause of suffering, and the veil of ignorance, which is the obstacle to omniscience) and who has brought to perfection the two sorts of knowledge (of the ultimate and relative nature of phenomena).

Buddhadharma: The teaching of the Buddha (see Dharma).

Chöd: (*chod*) Literally 'cutting.' A system of tantric meditation based on the teachings of the Prajñaparamita and introduced into Tibet by Padampa Sangye. It aims at the cutting through of all attachment to self.

Circumambulation: A highly meritorious devotional practice, consisting in walking clockwise, concentratedly and with awareness, around a sacred object, e.g. a temple, stupa, holy mountain, or the house, and even the person, of a spiritual master.

Dharma: (*chos*) The body of teaching expounded by the Buddha Shakyamuni and other enlightened beings which shows the way to enlightenment. It comprises two aspects: the Dharma of transmission (*lung gi chos*), namely the teachings which are actually given, and the Dharma of realization (*rtogs pa'i chos*), or the states of wisdom etc, which are attained through the application of the teachings.

Dharmakaya: (*chos sku*) The absolute, or truth, body; the aspect of emptiness.

Dzogchen: (*rdzogs chen*) (Skt: Mahasandhi, Atiyoga) The Great Perfection, the highest view according to the Nyingmapa tradition.

Eighteen characteristics of a precious human existence: These eighteen characteristics comprise eight freedoms and ten endowments. The eight freedoms consist in not being born, 1) in the realms of Hell, 2) as a hungry ghost, 3) as an animal, 4) in the realms of the gods, 5) among barbarians who are ignorant of the teachings and practices of the Buddhadharma, 6) as one with wrong views such as those of nihilism or of the substantiality of the ego and phenomena etc., 7) in a time or place where a Buddha has not appeared and 8) as mentally handicapped. The ten endowments are subdivided into five which are considered as intrinsic, and five as extrinsic, to the personality. The five intrinsic endowments are 1) to be born as a human being, 2) to inhabit a 'central land', i.e. where the Buddhadharma is proclaimed, 3) to be in possession of normal faculties, 4) to be one who has not abandoned himself to great karmic negativity and 5) to have faith in the Dharma. The five extrinsic endowments are the facts that 1) a Buddha has appeared in the world, 2) that he has expounded the Doctrine, 3) that his Doctrine still persists, 4) that it is practised and 5) that one is accepted as a disciple by a spiritual master.

Kadampa: Lineage of Tibetan Buddhism deriving from the teachings of Atisha (982-1054). Its teaching emphasizes monastic discipline, study and the practice of compassion. The influence of the Kadampa tradition is pervasive in all schools of Tibetan Buddhism although it is especially associated with the Gelugpa teaching, which indeed is sometimes referred to as the New Kadampa.

Kagyupa: One of the new schools of Tibetan Buddhism, founded by Marpa the Translator (1012-1095).

Kalpa: (*bskal pa*) Term given to immense periods of time as conceived in the traditional cosmology of India. A great kalpa, which corresponds to the period of formation, duration, disappearance and absence of a universal system, comprises eighty small kalpas. An intermediary kalpa consists of two small kalpas taken together, in the first of which the duration of life increases, while in the second it decreases.

Karma: Sanskrit word meaning 'action,' understood as the law of causality. According to the Buddha's teaching, all actions, whether of thought, word or deed, are like seeds which will eventually bear fruit in terms of experience, whether in this or future lives. A positive or virtuous act will result in happiness, while the definition of sin or negative action is that which is the cause of suffering for the agent later on.

Lower Realms: See glossary note on Samsara.

Mahamudra: (*phyag rgya chen po*) The Great Seal, the highest view according to the Kagyupa tradition.

Mala: A string of beads (usually 108) used as a counting aid in mantra recitation.

Mahayana: The Great Vehicle, see note under Shravaka-yana.

Mani: The mantra of Chenrezig, the six syllables 'Om Mani Padme Hung.'

Mantra: (*sngags*) Formula consisting of words or syllables associated with specific meditational deities, the recitation of which forms an essential part of tantric meditation.

Mantrayana: (*gsang sngags rdo rje theg pa*) The mantra vehicle, sometimes referred as the diamond vehicle or Vajrayana. The collection of teachings and practices based on the tantras, which though in fact an aspect of the Mahayana is sometimes considered as a separate vehicle. See note on Shravakayana.

Nirmanakaya: (*sprul sku*) The manifestation body, the aspect of compassion and means, whereby a Buddha may be perceived by unenlightened beings and the means therefore by which he can communicate with and help them.

Nirvana: (*myang ngan las 'das pa*) The Tibetan translation of this Sanskrit word means 'gone beyond suffering' and indicates the various levels of enlightenment gained according to the practice of the Shravakayana or Mahayana.

Nyingmapa: (*rnying ma pa*) The Ancients. The earliest school of Tibetan Buddhism founded in the eighth century by the Guru Padmasambhava.

Pratyekabuddha: (*rang sangs rgyas*) One who attains enlightenment alone, without the aid of a master, and who does not transmit teachings to others.

Pratimoksha: (*so sor thar pa*) Individual liberation: the seven sets of precepts for ordained and lay people according to the Buddhist discipline.

Pure field: (*gzhing khams*) see footnote 14

Rinpoche: (*rin po che*) Literally 'most precious one,' a form of address used in Tibetan Buddhism for Incarnate Lamas, Abbots and respected teachers.

Sadhana: (*sgrub thabs*) A ritual, or text of a ritual, serving as a support for meditation in the Mantrayana.

Sambhogakaya: (*longs sku*) The Body of Enjoyment, the transhuman form in which a Buddha may manifest himself, directly perceptible only to highly realized beings.

Samsara: (*'khor ba*) The wheel or round of existence; the state of being unenlightened in which the mind, enslaved by the three poisons of Desire, Anger and Ignorance, evolves uncontrolled from one state to another, passing through an endless stream of psycho-physical experiences all of which are characterized by suffering. See entry on the Six Realms.

Shravakayana/Hinayana: The practitioners of Dharma are identified as belonging to two different sets of teaching or 'vehicles', according to the nature of their aspirations. These are known as the Hinayana, or Root Vehicle, and the Mahayana, or Great Vehicle. The Root Vehicle is subdivided into the way of the Hearers (or Shravakas), disciples of the Buddha, and the way of those who seek enlightenment relying only on themselves, or Pratyekabuddhas. The goal of the Shravaka and Pratyekabuddha paths is nirvana, conceived of as definitive liberation from the sufferings of samsara. The Great Vehicle is that of the Bodhisattvas, those who, while accepting the validity and efficacy of the other vehicle, aspire to the full enlightenment of Buddhahood for the sake of all beings. The term Hinayana is frequently taken to be pejorative and for that reason is often avoided. Numerous masters, e.g. His Holiness the Dalai Lama and Nyanaponika Mahathera, suggest that 'Shravakayana' be used instead, even though, at least here, the category is understood to include the Pratyekabuddhas as well.

Six Realms: (*'gro drug*) The experience of beings in samsara is traditionally schematized into six general categories, referred to as realms or worlds, in which the mind abides as the result of previous actions or karma. None of these states is satisfactory, though the degree of suffering in them differs from one to another. The three upper or fortunate realms, where suffering is alleviated by temporary pleasures, are the heavens of the mundane gods, the realms of the Asuras or demigods, and the world of human beings. The three lower realms, in which suffering predominates over every other experience, are those of the animals, the hungry ghosts, and the hells.

Six Transcendent Perfections: (*Skt. Paramita; Tbt. pha rol tu phyin pa*) The six activities of generosity, moral discipline, patience, enthusiasm, meditation and wisdom, which form the practice of the Bodhisattva path.

Sugatagarbha: (*bde gshegs snying po*) see Tathagatagarbha.

Sutrayana: The Mahayana has two subsections: the sutrayana, i.e. the teachings based on the sutras and propounding the practice of the six transcendent perfections; and the mantrayana, the teachings and practices based on the tantra texts.

Svabhavikakaya: (*ngo bo nyid sku*) The Essential Body, the aspect of inseparability of the three other bodies.

Tathagatagarbha: (*de bzhin gshegs pa'i snying po*) The Buddha-nature, the potential for Buddhahood, present in the mind of every sentient being.

Three Trainings: (*bslab pa gsum*) i.e. Discipline, Concentration and Wisdom.

Three Jewels/Triple Jewel: (*dkon mchog gsum*) i.e. The Buddha, the Doctrine (Dharma) and the Assembly of disciples and practitioners (Sangha). These are the three objects of refuge.

Torma: (*gtor ma*) A sort of ritual cake of varying shape and composition, used in practices and rituals of the Mantrayana. Depending on the circumstances, it is considered as an offering, a representation or mandala of the meditational deity, or even a kind of symbolic weapon in ceremonies to remove obstacles from the path.

Vipashyana: (*lhag mthong*) Penetrative Insight meditation which reveals the absence of inherent existence in both the mind and phenomena.

Wheel of Dharma: The symbol of the Buddha's teaching. The Dharma is divided into three broad categories, traditionally known as the Three Turnings of the Wheel of the Dharma. The First Turning of the Wheel corresponds to the Buddha's first teachings on the Four Noble Truths of suffering and the release from suffering. The Second Turning consists of teachings on emptiness: the doctrine that all phenomena are devoid of self-entity and true existence. The Third Turning comprises teachings on the Tathagatagarbha, or Buddha-nature inherent in the minds of all sentient beings.

Yidam deity: (*yi dam*) A form of a Buddha used as a support in visualisation and meditation in the Mantrayana. Such deities may be masculine or feminine, peaceful or wrathful, regarded ultimately as being inseparable from the mind of the meditator.